Pizza modo mio
John Lanzafame

THANKS A really big thanks to Peter Evans for opening doors for me — and keeping them open. He is a true friend and I call him 'mate'. I could never have done it without him.

Thanks to my manager Lisa Sullivan who gave me a great boost of confidence.

Thanks to Glen Austin — a real chef who has taken me places I never thought I could go. Thanks also to the 2008 Australian Culinary Olympic team: Rick Stephens, Peter Wright, Neil Abrahams, Andre Kropp, Shannon Kellam, Adrian Tobin, Shane Keighley, Matt McBain and Gary Farrell. These guys push for culinary excellence and have brought me to food that is truly world class.

Thank you to all the people at Murdoch Books who have persevered with my endless questions and spelling mistakes to bring my first book to such a high standard. Thank you Jane, Hugh, Kate, Alan, Christine and Paul — there is no way this book could have got there without all our minds acting as one.

To Justine, Isabella and Dante — without their support and sleepless nights with me working, I could never win any of the accolades I have in my life. They are the greatest, precious and most loving people in my life **TI AMO PER SEMPRE**.

Published in 2008 by Murdoch Books Pty Limited

Murdoch Books Australia
Pier 8/9, 23 Hickson Road
Millers Point NSW 2000
Phone: +61 (0) 2 8220 2000
Fax: +61 (0) 2 8220 2558
www.murdochbooks.com.au

Murdoch Books UK Limited
Erico House, 6th Floor
93–99 Upper Richmond Road
Putney, London SW15 2TG
Phone: +44 (0) 20 8785 5995
Fax: +44 (0) 20 8785 5985
www.murdochbooks.co.uk

Printed by 1010 Printing International Ltd in 2008
PRINTED IN CHINA.

Chief Executive: Juliet Rogers
Publishing Director: Kay Scarlett

Commissioning Editor: Jane Lawson
Editor: Paul McNally
Design Concept and Layout: Hugh Ford
Food Editor: Christine Osmond
Photographer: Alan Benson
Stylist: Kate Brown
Production: Nikla Martin

National Library of Australia Cataloguing-in-Publication Data:
Lanzafame, John
Pizza modo mio
Includes index.
ISBN 978 1 741962 031 (pbk.)
Cookery.
Pizza.
641.8248

Pizza modo mio
John Lanzafame

MURDOCH BOOKS

Contents

6 Introduction

When I hear the words 'pizza champion', I just laugh – it was a role I fell into by accident. I had sold my restaurant Lanzafame and started working at GPO in Sydney's Martin Place, where I was quite content to be back in the kitchen. One morning Spiro, the restaurant manager, came in and said that the pizza chef was running late. So, I went over to set up, thinking to myself 'How hard can this be? I'm Italian after all!' Spiro was already in a panic and was off drinking coffee somewhere to calm down. I piled the wood in the oven, fired it up and found some dough that was in the refrigerator. Menu in hand, away I went. What I remember of that day is Spiro walking past and saying 'You know how to cook pizza!' – and that's how it all started.

About six months later I joined the Hugo's group as executive chef at the Kings Cross, Sydney, venue. Peter Evans, the chef and owner, asked if I would join him to put a personal stamp on his eatery. After only three weeks on the job, Peter called me over and told me he'd entered the Dairy Farmers Best of the Best Pizza competition, but now he couldn't make it – 'So,' he asked, 'would you step in for me?' I couldn't say no.

Without holding any expectations, I entered the competition for the best pizza in NSW and – to my suprise – I won! After winning the state final, I was off to compete in the national finals. The morning of the competition, I was thinking 'How the hell did I get here?' I'd only been cooking pizzas for a short while and was now competing with the best five pizza chefs in Australia, who beat out 1000 other competitors. And then, unexpectedly, I won the Australian competition too – with a fresh salmon, red onion and fried caper pizza.

After winning the national prize, I travelled to New York to compete in The America's Plate – the most prestigious award for pizza in the US. Here you compete against some of the best pizza chefs from around the world. I had the benefit of being able to talk to Glen Austin before the competition kicked off. Glen, an Australian pizza judge and the chairman of that year's competition, had never met me previously and had no idea that my pizza experience stemmed from less than a year on the job. But my ideas were heard and agreed upon by everyone – Glen, Peter Evans and the rest of the team. So that morning in New York, competing against pizza chefs from across the world, I won best pizza, selected by a panel of ten judges. I was very proud indeed. My winning pizza remains one of my all-time favourites – filled river calamari (you'll find this one on page 74).

My pizza philosophy is simple – less is more. Concentrate on one flavour, rather than a bunch of different ones. I would much rather make a lot of little pizzas, using a few key ingredients, than just one big pizza with everything piled on top. Also, the dough should be thin and crispy – not thick, tasteless and soggy. I have travelled to enough places to know that people really do prefer a thin and crispy base.

I often find myself using ingredients that are leftovers from the night before. Again, simplicity here is important. One of my favourite 'leftover' pizzas uses bolognaise sauce on a base of mozzarella, which is cooked and topped with some freshly shaved parmesan. This is a no-fuss, simple to prepare and, most of all, tasty pizza.

I hope you enjoy *Pizza modo mio* – it is truly from my heart. Pizza has taken me places that I would never have imagined I would have gone and helped to create many lasting friendships.

Basics

Following are some of the staples I use in my work kitchen and at home. Most of the recipes were taught to me by my mother; others I picked up along the way from fellow chefs and friends. Many of these basics can also be used in other recipes, such as pasta sauces. Having a stock of basics means saving time in food preparation – and saving time in the kitchen means more time with the family, which means everything to me.

Plain dough

Makes 170 g (6 oz) dough (enough for one 30 cm/12 inch pizza)

1 teaspoon dried yeast
1 teaspoon salt
100 ml (3^1/$_2$ fl oz) warm water
2 teaspoons olive oil, plus extra, for greasing
160 g (5^1/$_2$ oz) plain (all-purpose) flour, sifted

Put the yeast, salt and warm water in a small bowl and whisk until just combined. Gradually whisk in the olive oil, then leave in a warm place for 10 minutes, or until the mixture starts to bubble.

Add the flour and knead for 15 minutes, or until the dough is smooth and elastic. Rub the inside of a large bowl with olive oil. Roll the dough around in the bowl to coat it with oil, then place in the bowl, cover with a clean cloth and leave in a draught-free spot for 1–1^1/$_2$ hours, or until doubled in size.

Punch down the dough to expel trapped air. (At this stage, the dough can be covered in plastic wrap and refrigerated overnight or frozen. Bring back to room temperature before continuing.) Place the dough on a baking tray lined with baking paper, cover and leave in a draught-free spot for 15 minutes, or until risen by half again. The dough is now ready to use.

Parmesan dough

Omit 50 g (1³/₄ oz) plain (all-purpose) flour from the plain dough recipe (page 12), then make the dough as per the recipe. When the dough has come together, add 50 g (1³/₄ oz/¹/₂ cup) grated parmesan cheese and knead until smooth and elastic.

Fresh herb dough

After the first rise and knock down of the plain dough (page 12), add ¹/₄ teaspoon finely chopped fresh soft herbs, such as basil, chervil, flat-leaf (Italian) parsley or chives, and knead briefly and continue as per the recipe. (Don't add them to the mixture before kneading or it will change the colour of the dough.)

Wholemeal dough

Replace the plain (all-purpose) flour in the plain dough recipe (page 12) with wholemeal plain (all-purpose) flour and continue as per the recipe.

Sweet dough

To create a caramelised crust, after the first rise and knock down of the plain dough (page 12), add 1 teaspoon soft brown sugar to the dough, knead briefly then continue as per the recipe.

Gluten-free dough

Makes two quantities 170 g (6 oz) dough (enough for two 30 cm/12 inch pizzas)

40 g (1^1/$_2$ oz) cornflour (cornstarch)
40 g (1^1/$_2$ oz) rice flour
40 g (1^1/$_2$ oz) tapioca flour
40 g (1^1/$_2$ oz) fine yellow polenta, plus extra, for dusting
^{1}/$_4$ teaspoon bicarbonate of soda (baking soda)
1 tablespoon salt
2 eggs, lightly beaten
85 ml (2^3/$_4$ fl oz) olive oil
125 ml (4 fl oz/^{1}/$_2$ cup) sparkling mineral water

Place all the dry ingredients in an electric mixer fitted with a dough hook and mix well.

With the mixer on low speed, gradually add the combined eggs, oil and mineral water and knead for 10 minutes. Divide the dough in half, place on a baking tray lined with baking paper, cover with plastic wrap and refrigerate for 1 hour.

Dust two pieces of baking paper with polenta, then roll out each portion of dough on the baking paper into a 30 cm (12 inch) round. Place a pizza tray over the top of each round, and flip over very gently (this dough is very fragile since it has no gluten).

Once the bases are rolled, they can be covered in plastic wrap and frozen for up to 2 months. Bases can then be used straight from the freezer without needing to defrost them.

Basic pizza sauce

Makes 250 ml (9 fl oz/1 cup)

250 ml (9 fl oz/1 cup) tinned chopped Italian tomatoes
1 small handful basil or oregano leaves

Put the tomatoes and basil or oregano in a food processor, season to taste, then blend until smooth. This sauce can be stored in the fridge for up to 5 days or frozen for up to 3 months.

Rich tomato ragu

Makes about 1 litre (35 fl oz/4 cups)

1 tablespoon olive oil
1 small brown onion, finely chopped
1 garlic clove, thinly sliced
500 g (1 lb 2 oz) veal shank (osso bucco cut)
125 ml (4 fl oz/$1/2$ cup) dry red wine
500 ml (17 fl oz/2 cups) tinned chopped Italian tomatoes

Heat the olive oil in a heavy-based saucepan over medium heat, add the onion and garlic and cook for 3–4 minutes, or until the onion is transparent. Add the veal shank and cook for another 5 minutes, or until browned, then add the wine and simmer until nearly evaporated. Add the tomatoes and 250 ml (9 fl oz/1 cup) water, reduce the heat to low and simmer very gently for 2 hours, or until the meat is just starting to fall off the bone.

Remove the meat from the sauce, discard the bones and shred the meat, then return the meat to the sauce and season to taste. This sauce can be stored in the fridge for up to 5 days or frozen for up to 3 months.

Black or green olive tapenade

Makes 250 ml (9 fl oz/1 cup)

40 g (1¹/₂ oz/¹/₃ cup) pitted green or black olives
2 tablespoons olive oil, plus extra, to cover
4 anchovy fillets
2 tablespoons onion confit (page 22)
2 tablespoons garlic confit (page 24)
1 tablespoon chilli confit (page 24)
3 tablespoons chopped flat-leaf (Italian) parsley

Put all the ingredients in a blender or mortar with a pestle and purée or pound until fine, then season to taste. Put in a small container and cover the surface with a thin layer of oil. This tapenade will keep, refrigerated, for up to 1 month. After using, cover the surface of the tapenade with another thin layer of oil to prevent it from oxidising.

Shellfish glaze

Makes 500 ml (17 fl oz/2 cups)

1 tablespoon olive oil
1 kg (2 lb 4 oz) black mussels, pipis, clams or vongole, cleaned and rinsed
250 ml (9 fl oz/1 cup) dry white wine
250 ml (9 fl oz/1 cup) cream

Heat the oil in a heavy-based saucepan over high heat, add the shellfish and wine, cover and cook, shaking the pan frequently, for 4–6 minutes, or just until the shells open. Pour the shellfish into a colander placed over a bowl and remove the meat, discarding any unopened shells.

Return the shellfish liquid to the pan, add the cream and simmer over low heat until reduced by two-thirds. Return the shellfish meat to the sauce, combine well and season to taste with freshly ground black pepper, then process in a blender until smooth.

Onion confit

Makes 375 ml (13 fl oz/1 1/2 cups)

2 small brown onions, finely chopped
150 ml (5 fl oz) olive oil

Preheat the oven to 120°C (235°F/Gas 1/2). Put the onion and oil in a small ovenproof dish and bake for 2 hours, making sure the onion does not colour. Remove from the oven, cool, then spoon into a 375 ml (13 fl oz/1 1/2 cup) capacity sterilised jar, seal and refrigerate for up to 3 months.

Balsamic onions

Makes 125 ml (4 fl oz/1/2 cup)

1 tablespoon olive oil
1 brown onion, thinly sliced
1 1/2 tablespoons soft brown sugar
4 tablespoons balsamic vinegar

Heat the oil in a heavy-based frying pan over high heat, add the onion and cook for 5 minutes, or until just starting to caramelise. Add the sugar and stir until dissolved, then add the balsamic vinegar, combine well and simmer over low heat for 6 minutes, or until the mixture is jam-like but not too dry. Balsamic onions can be stored in an airtight container in the fridge for up to 10 days.

Chilli confit

Makes 250 ml (9 fl oz/1 cup)

350 g (12 oz) fresh long red or green chillies (about 16), halved, seeded and thinly sliced
150 ml (5 fl oz) olive oil

Preheat the oven to 120°C (235°F/Gas ¹/₂). Put the chillies and oil in a small ovenproof dish and bake for 2 hours, making sure the chilli does not colour. Remove from the oven, cool, then store in a 250 ml (9 fl oz/1 cup) capacity sterilised jar, seal and refrigerate for up to 3 months.

Garlic confit

Makes 250 ml (9 fl oz/1 cup)

200 g (7 oz) garlic cloves (about 30), peeled
150 ml (5 fl oz) olive oil

Preheat the oven to 120°C (235°F/Gas ¹/₂). Put the garlic and oil in a small ovenproof dish and bake for 2 hours, making sure the garlic does not colour. Remove from the oven, cool, then store in a 250 ml (9 fl oz/1 cup) capacity sterilised jar, seal and refrigerate for up to 3 months.

Green chilli purée

Makes 500 ml (17 fl oz/2 cups)

250 ml (9 fl oz/1 cup) olive oil
1 brown onion, finely chopped
2 tablespoons chopped fresh herbs including thyme, basil and rosemary
300 g (10¹/₂ oz) fresh long green chillies, seeded and chopped

Preheat the oven to 180°C (350°F/Gas 4). Heat the olive oil in a heavy-based ovenproof frying pan over low heat, add the onion and herbs and cook over low heat for 6–8 minutes, or until soft. Add the chillies and cook over medium heat until light golden. Transfer the pan to the oven and bake until tender, then purée until smooth and season to taste.

Pesto – modo mio

Makes 500 ml (17 fl oz/2 cups)

Juice of 1 lemon
2 large handfuls basil
2 tablespoons pine nuts, toasted
2 anchovy fillets
3 tablespoons grated parmesan cheese
80 ml (2$^1/_2$ fl oz/$^1/_3$ cup) olive oil, plus extra, to cover
1 tablespoon onion confit (page 22)
1 tablespoon garlic confit (page 24)

Put all the ingredients in a mortar or food processor and pound or blend until smooth. Season to taste, pour into a jar and cover with a thin layer of olive oil. This pesto will keep, refrigerated, for up to 1 month. After using, cover the surface of the pesto with another thin layer of oil to prevent it from oxidising.

Poor man's parmesan

Makes about 1 cup

1 cup torn stale sourdough bread
4 tablespoons olive oil
2 anchovy fillets, chopped
1 large handful chopped flat-leaf (Italian) parsley

Put the torn bread in a food processor and process until coarse breadcrumbs form. Heat the oil in a frying pan over medium heat, add the anchovy fillets and allow to dissolve in the oil before adding the parsley. Fry for 30 seconds then add the breadcrumbs to the pan, mixing through until well combined, crisp and golden.

Lemon dressing

Makes 3 tablespoons

1 tablespoon lemon juice
2 tablespoons extra virgin olive oil

Put the lemon juice and oil in a small sealable jar, season to taste with sea salt and freshly ground black pepper and shake until well combined.

Mayonnaise

Makes 250 ml (9 fl oz/1 cup)

1 egg yolk, at room temperature
1 tablespoon dijon mustard
2 tablespoons lemon juice
250 ml (9 fl oz/1 cup) vegetable oil, or half olive and half vegetable oil, at room temperature

Put the egg yolk, mustard and lemon juice in a small bowl and whisk to combine well. Whisking continuously, gradually add the oil, drop by drop at first, then in a thin steady stream, until the mixture is very thick. Season to taste.

For anchovy mayonnaise, use 1 teaspoon dijon mustard and add 3 finely chopped anchovy fillets to the yolks.

Traditional pizzas

'Traditional' is a term that I use loosely, as there is not an official register of 'traditional' pizzas – nor is one man's 'margherita' like another. However, the pizzas in this chapter are those that have been a popular fixture on the pizza scene for longer than I can remember. They are simple, tasty and popular – and you're likely to find them all on any good pizza menu in the world. The simplicity in these original pizzas is what inspires me in my pizza creations today. I owe a debt of gratitude to the multitude of pizza chefs that created these 'iconic' recipes long before me.

Plain pizza bread

Makes one 30 cm (12 inch) pizza

Coarse semolina, for dusting
1 quantity pizza dough (page 12)
3 tablespoons extra virgin olive oil
Sea salt, to season

Place a pizza stone or heavy-based oven tray in the oven and preheat to 250°C (500°F/Gas 9).

Lightly dust your workbench with semolina, then roll out the dough into a 30 cm (12 inch) round, place on a pizza tray and prod the base with your finger until dented all over. Drizzle with the olive oil and sprinkle generously with sea salt, then place on the preheated stone or tray and bake for 5–6 minutes, or until the base is golden and crisp.

Garlic pizza

Makes one 30 cm (12 inch) pizza

Coarse semolina, for dusting
1 quantity pizza dough (page 12)
$1/4$ quantity garlic confit (page 24), puréed until smooth
1 tablespoon extra virgin olive oil, plus extra, for drizzling
50 g (1$3/4$ oz/$1/3$ cup) grated mozzarella cheese
2 tablespoons chopped flat-leaf (Italian) parsley
Sea salt, to season

Place a pizza stone or heavy-based oven tray in the oven and preheat to 250°C (500°F/Gas 9).

Lightly dust your workbench with semolina, then roll out the dough into a 30 cm (12 inch) round, place on a pizza tray and prod the base with your finger until dented all over. Spread the base with the garlic confit purée, drizzle with the olive oil, then scatter with the mozzarella and parsley and season to taste with sea salt. Place on the preheated stone or tray and bake for 5–6 minutes, or until the base is golden and crisp. Remove from the oven, drizzle with a little more oil and serve.

Margherita pizza

Makes one 30 cm (12 inch) pizza

Coarse semolina, for dusting
1 quantity pizza dough (page 12)
$^1/_2$ quantity basic pizza sauce (page 18)
1 tablespoon chopped flat-leaf (Italian) parsley
75 g (2$^1/_2$ oz/$^1/_2$ cup) grated mozzarella cheese
180 g (6$^1/_4$ oz) cherry tomatoes, thinly sliced
6 basil leaves
40 g (1$^1/_2$ oz) buffalo mozzarella cheese, torn into 6 pieces
3 tablespoons grated parmesan cheese

Place a pizza stone or heavy-based oven tray in the oven and preheat to 250°C (500°F/Gas 9).

Lightly dust your workbench with semolina, then roll out the dough into a 30 cm (12 inch) round, place on a pizza tray and prick all over with a fork. Spread the pizza sauce over the base and scatter with the parsley, grated mozzarella and tomatoes. Place the tray on the preheated stone or tray and bake for 5–6 minutes, or until the base is golden and crisp.

Remove from the oven, top with basil leaves, buffalo mozzarella pieces, sprinkle with grated parmesan and serve.

Pepperoni pizza

Makes one 30 cm (12 inch) pizza

Coarse semolina, for dusting
1 quantity pizza dough (page 12)
$1/2$ quantity basic pizza sauce (page 18)
2 tablespoons chopped flat-leaf (Italian) parsley
1 roma (plum) tomato, thinly sliced
50 g ($1^3/4$ oz/$1/3$ cup) grated mozzarella cheese
100 g ($3^1/2$ oz) thinly sliced pepperoni
6 mint leaves
40 g ($1^1/2$ oz) buffalo mozzarella cheese, torn into 6 pieces

Place a pizza stone or heavy-based oven tray in the oven and preheat to 250°C (500°F/Gas 9).

Lightly dust your workbench with semolina, then roll out the dough into a 30 cm (12 inch) round, place on a pizza tray and prick all over with a fork. Spread the pizza sauce over the base, then scatter with the parsley, tomato, mozzarella and pepperoni in that order. Place the tray on the preheated stone or tray and cook for 5–6 minutes, or until the base is golden and crisp.

Remove from the oven, cut into 6 wedges, then top each wedge with a mint leaf and a piece of buffalo mozzarella.

Double-smoked ham pizza

Makes one 30 cm (12 inch) pizza

2 tablespoons olive oil
150 g (5$^1/_2$ oz) small field mushrooms, thinly sliced
2 tablespoons balsamic vinegar
2 tablespoons caster (superfine) sugar
Coarse semolina, for dusting
1 quantity pizza dough (page 12)
$^1/_2$ quantity basic pizza sauce (page 18)
2 tablespoons chopped flat-leaf (Italian) parsley
75 g (2$^1/_2$ oz/$^1/_2$ cup) grated mozzarella cheese
70 g (2$^1/_2$ oz/$^1/_2$ cup) torn double-smoked ham
30 g (1 oz) taleggio cheese

Heat the olive oil in a heavy-based frying pan over high heat, add the mushrooms and cook for 4–5 minutes, or until golden. Remove from the heat and season to taste.

Meanwhile, put the balsamic vinegar and sugar in a small saucepan and simmer over low heat until reduced by two-thirds. Remove from the heat and set aside.

Place a pizza stone or heavy-based oven tray in the oven and preheat to 250°C (500°F/Gas 9).

Lightly dust your workbench with semolina, then roll out the dough into a 30 cm (12 inch) round, place on a pizza tray and prick all over with a fork. Spread the pizza sauce over the base, then scatter with the parsley, mozzarella, mushrooms and ham in that order. Tear the taleggio into small pieces and scatter over the top, then place the tray on the preheated stone or tray and bake for 5–6 minutes, or until the base is golden and crisp. Remove from the oven, drizzle with the reduced balsamic vinegar and serve.

Potato, anchovy, rosemary and white prosciutto pizza

Makes one 30 cm (12 inch) pizza

Coarse semolina, for dusting
1 quantity pizza dough (page 12)
1 tablespoon olive oil
10 thin slices white prosciutto (lardo)
4 anchovy fillets
1 large desiree potato, unpeeled, cut into wafer-thin slices
2 teaspoons rosemary sprigs
75 g (2^1/$_2$ oz/^{1}/$_2$ cup) grated mozzarella cheese
3 tablespoons shaved pecorino cheese
3 garlic confit cloves (page 24), each cut into 4

Place a pizza stone or heavy-based oven tray in the oven and preheat to 250°C (500°F/Gas 9).

Lightly dust your workbench with semolina, then roll out the dough into a 30 cm (12 inch) round, place on a pizza tray and prick all over with a fork. Drizzle the oil over the base, then scatter with the prosciutto and anchovy fillets. Place the potato over the top, in slightly overlapping layers, scatter with the rosemary sprigs, cheeses and garlic confit in that order. Place on the preheated stone or tray and bake for 5–8 minutes, or until the base is golden and crisp.

This pizza can also be served with slices of leftover roast lamb scattered over the top.

Puttanesca pizza

Makes one 30 cm (12 inch) pizza

Coarse semolina, for dusting
1 quantity pizza dough (page 12)
$^1/_2$ quantity basic pizza sauce (page 18)
180 g (6$^1/_4$ oz) cherry tomatoes, thinly sliced
1 tablespoon capers
3 tablespoons pitted black or green olives
4 anchovy fillets
1 tablespoon chopped flat-leaf (Italian) parsley
1 tablespoon garlic confit (page 24), finely chopped
75 g (2$^1/_2$ oz/$^1/_2$ cup) grated mozzarella cheese

Place a pizza stone or heavy-based oven tray in the oven and preheat to 250°C (500°F/Gas 9).

Lightly dust your workbench with semolina, then roll out the dough into a 30 cm (12 inch) round, place on a pizza tray and prick all over with a fork. Spread the base with the pizza sauce, then scatter with the remaining ingredients and season to taste. Place on the preheated stone or tray and bake for 5–6 minutes, or until the base is golden and crisp.

Prosciutto pizza

Makes one 30 cm (12 inch) pizza

Coarse semolina, for dusting
1 quantity pizza dough (page 12)
$^1/_2$ quantity basic pizza sauce (page 18)
75 g ($2^1/_2$ oz/$^1/_2$ cup) grated mozzarella cheese
6 basil leaves
1 roma (plum) tomato, thinly sliced
6 slices prosciutto
1 large handful rocket (arugula) leaves
2 tablespoons extra virgin olive oil
1 tablespoon balsamic vinegar
35 g ($1^1/_4$ oz/$^1/_3$ cup) shaved parmesan cheese

Place a pizza stone or heavy-based oven tray in the oven and preheat to 250°C (500°F/Gas 9).

Lightly dust your workbench with semolina, then roll out the dough into a 30 cm (12 inch) round, place on a pizza tray and prick all over with a fork. Spread the base with pizza sauce and scatter with the mozzarella, basil and tomato, then place on the preheated stone or tray and bake for 5–6 minutes, or until the base is golden and crisp.

Remove from the oven and lay the prosciutto over the top. Toss the rocket leaves in a bowl with the olive oil and balsamic vinegar, season to taste, scatter over the prosciutto, then sprinkle with the shaved parmesan and serve.

Pescatore pizza

Makes one 30 cm (12 inch) pizza

2 tablespoons olive oil
10 black mussels, cleaned
100 g (3^1/$_2$ oz) baby octopus, cleaned and cut into 2 cm (^{3}/$_4$ inch) pieces
10 raw small prawns (shrimp), peeled and deveined
60 g (2^1/$_4$ oz) skinless firm white fish fillet, cut into 1 cm (^{1}/$_2$ inch) pieces
1 river calamari, cleaned and cut into 5 mm (^{1}/$_4$ inch) thick rings, tentacles reserved
2 tablespoons chopped flat-leaf (Italian) parsley
^{1}/$_2$ quantity basic pizza sauce (page 18)
Coarse semolina, for dusting
1 quantity pizza dough (page 12)
75 g (2^1/$_2$ oz/^{1}/$_2$ cup) grated mozzarella cheese
Lemon wedges, to serve

Heat 1 tablespoon of the olive oil in a large heavy-based frying pan, add the mussels, cover and shake the pan over high heat for 3 minutes, or just until the shells open. Pour into a colander over a bowl (reserving the juices) and, when cool enough to handle, remove the meat from the shells. Discard any unopened mussels.

Return the pan to the heat, add the remaining oil, then add the calamari rings and tentacles, prawns, fish and octopus and toss over high heat for 2 minutes, or until nearly cooked through. Add the parsley and season to taste, then pour the seafood into a colander placed over a bowl and return the pan to the heat. Add the pizza sauce and any juices from the seafood (including the mussel juices) and simmer over low heat for 6 minutes, or until slightly thickened.

Place a pizza stone or heavy-based oven tray in the oven and preheat to 250°C (500°F/Gas 9).

Lightly dust your workbench with semolina, then roll out the dough into a 30 cm (12 inch) round, place on a pizza tray and prick all over with a fork. Spread the base with the pizza sauce, scatter with the mozzarella, then the seafood. Place on the preheated stone or tray and bake for 5–6 minutes, or until the base is golden and crisp. Serve with lemon wedges for squeezing over.

Capricciosa pizza

Makes one 30 cm (12 inch) pizza

2 tablespoons olive oil
100 g (3¹/₂ oz) oyster mushrooms
Coarse semolina, for dusting
1 quantity pizza dough (page 12)
1 roma (plum) tomato, thinly sliced
1 tablespoon chilli confit (page 24)
100 g (3¹/₂ oz) smoked chicken, chopped
3 tablespoons pitted kalamata olives
60 g (2¹/₄ oz) buffalo mozzarella cheese, torn
1 handful basil leaves
35 g (1¹/₄ oz/¹/₃ cup) shaved parmesan cheese
2 tablespoons anchovy mayonnaise (page 28)

Heat the olive oil in a heavy-based frying pan over high heat and, when very hot, add the mushrooms and cook for 3–4 minutes, or until the mushrooms are just tender. Remove from the pan, drain well, then season to taste.

Place a pizza stone or heavy-based oven tray in the oven and preheat to 250°C (500°F/Gas 9).

Lightly dust your workbench with semolina, then roll out the dough into a 30 cm (12 inch) round, place on a pizza tray and prick all over with a fork. Spread the tomato over the base, drizzle with the chilli confit, then scatter over the smoked chicken, oyster mushrooms, olives, mozzarella and basil in that order. Place on the preheated stone or tray and bake for 5–6 minutes, or until the base is golden and crisp.

Remove from the oven, scatter with the shaved parmesan, then drizzle with the anchovy mayonnaise and serve.

Modo mio

Modo mio, or 'my style', are the pizzas that
tell you about me and my style of food.
In this chapter you'll find all my favourites –
simple and satisfying recipes with ingredients
that I love to use on a day-to-day basis.
I'm sure you'll love them too – but feel free
to make them *modo vostro*, 'your style'.
In fashion true to my origins, these recipes
are very Italian – Southern Italian – where
the style is simple and the ingredients rich in
flavour. Like all pizzas, these should be made
with lots of family and friends around to join
in the fun of making and eating them.

Mum's favourite fried porcini pizza

Makes one 30 cm (12 inch) pizza

3 tablespoons olive oil
150 g (5^1/$_2$ oz) button mushrooms
3 garlic cloves, thinly sliced
1 French shallot, thinly sliced
2 teaspoons finely chopped fresh long red chillies, seeded
70 g (2^1/$_2$ oz/^{1}/$_2$ cup) sliced fresh porcini mushrooms
50 g (1^3/$_4$ oz/^{1}/$_3$ cup) grated mozzarella cheese
Coarse semolina, for dusting
1 quantity parmesan dough (page 14)
30 g (1 oz/^{1}/$_3$ cup) shaved truffled pecorino picante cheese
10 g (^{1}/$_4$ oz) fresh black truffle, thinly shaved

Heat 1 tablespoon of the olive oil in a heavy-based frying pan over high heat, add the button mushrooms and half the garlic, shallot and chilli and toss for 8 minutes, or until golden. Remove the mushroom mixture from the pan, season to taste, then purée in a food processor or blender until smooth.

Wipe the pan clean, then heat the remaining oil, add the porcini mushrooms and the remaining garlic, shallot and chilli and toss over medium heat for 5–8 minutes, or until the porcini are just golden. Remove from the heat and season to taste.

Place a pizza stone or heavy-based oven tray in the oven and preheat to 250°C (500°F/Gas 9).

Lightly dust your workbench with semolina, then roll out the dough into a 30 cm (12 inch) round, place on a pizza tray and prick all over with a fork. Spread the base with the mushroom purée, then scatter with mozzarella and the fried porcini. Place on the preheated stone or tray and bake for 5–8 minutes, or until the base is golden and crisp. Remove from the oven, scatter with the shaved pecorino and black truffle and serve.

Fried sicilian tomatoes and parmigiano reggiano pizza

Makes one 30 cm (12 inch) pizza

Fried Sicilian tomato sauce
80 ml (2¹/₂ fl oz/¹/₃ cup) olive oil
1 brown onion, thinly sliced
4 garlic cloves, thinly sliced
2 green or red ox-heart tomatoes, sliced

Coarse semolina, for dusting
1 quantity pizza dough (page 12)
50 g (1³/₄ oz/¹/₃ cup) grated mozzarella cheese
35 g (1¹/₄ oz/¹/₃ cup) shaved Parmigiano Reggiano cheese

For the fried Sicilian tomato sauce, heat the olive oil in a heavy-based frying pan over medium heat, add the onion and garlic and cook for 5 minutes, or until golden. Add the tomatoes, reduce the heat to very low and cook, stirring frequently, for 10 minutes, or until the oil is just starting to separate and the mixture is thick like tomato paste (concentrated purée). Do not season the sauce as it will already be very rich and concentrated.

Place a pizza stone or heavy-based oven tray in the oven and preheat to 250°C (500°F/Gas 9).

Lightly dust your workbench with semolina, then roll out the dough into a 30 cm (12 inch) round, place on a pizza tray and prick all over with a fork. Spread half the Sicilian tomato sauce over the base (store the remaining sauce in an airtight container in the refrigerator for up to 1 week), then scatter with the mozzarella, place on the preheated stone or tray and bake for 5–8 minutes, or until the base is golden and crisp. Remove from the oven, scatter the Parmigiano over the top (especially the oily puddles!) and serve.

Asparagus with crushed walnuts and truffle oil pizza

Makes one 30 cm (12 inch) pizza

1 tablespoon olive oil
1 white onion, thinly sliced
Coarse semolina, for dusting
1 quantity pizza dough (page 12)
100 g (3^1/$_2$ oz/^{1}/$_2$ cup) goat's curd
2 tablespoons chopped flat-leaf (Italian) parsley
50 g (1^3/$_4$ oz/^{1}/$_3$ cup) grated mozzarella cheese
4 green asparagus spears, blanched
1 free-range egg
2 tablespoons grated parmesan cheese
1 tablespoon crushed toasted walnuts
3 tablespoons shaved parmesan cheese
1^1/$_2$ teaspoons white truffle oil

Place a pizza stone or heavy-based oven tray in the oven and preheat to 250°C (500°F/Gas 9).

Heat the olive oil in a heavy-based frying pan over high heat, add the onion and cook for 4–5 minutes, or until golden.

Lightly dust your workbench with semolina, then roll out the dough into a 30 cm (12 inch) round, place on a pizza tray and prick all over with a fork. Spread the goat's curd over the base, then scatter with the chopped parsley, cooked onion and mozzarella. Slice the asparagus in half lengthways and place over the pizza. Carefully crack the egg in the centre of the pizza and scatter with the grated parmesan, then place on the preheated pizza stone or tray and bake for 5–8 minutes, or until the base is golden and crisp. Remove from the oven, scatter with the crushed walnuts and shaved parmesan, drizzle with truffle oil and serve.

Pumpkin pizza

Makes one 30 cm (12 inch) pizza

3 tablespoons soft brown sugar
120 g (4^1/$_4$ oz) pumpkin, cut into 1 cm (^{1}/$_2$ inch) pieces
1 small handful rosemary sprigs
1 head of garlic, top sliced off and discarded
1 zucchini (courgette), cut lengthways into 2 mm (^{1}/$_{16}$ inch) thick slices
Olive oil, for brushing
Coarse semolina, for dusting
1 quantity pizza dough (page 12)
2 tablespoons pine nuts, toasted
2 tablespoons chopped flat-leaf (Italian) parsley
2 tablespoons balsamic onions (page 22)
30 g (1 oz) gorgonzola dolce latte cheese, crumbled
75 g (2^1/$_2$ oz/^{1}/$_2$ cup) grated mozzarella cheese

Place a pizza stone or heavy-based oven tray in the oven and preheat to 180°C (350°F/Gas 4).

Combine the pumpkin, brown sugar, rosemary and garlic in a heavy-based roasting pan and roast for 15 minutes, or until golden and tender.

Put the zucchini slices on a heavy-based oven tray in a single layer, brush with a little olive oil and season to taste, then bake for 2–3 minutes, or until just tender.

Increase the oven temperature to 250°C (500°F/Gas 9).

Lightly dust your workbench with semolina, then roll out the dough into a 30 cm (12 inch) round, place on a pizza tray and prick all over with a fork. Brush the base with oil, then scatter with the pine nuts, parsley and balsamic onions. Top with the zucchini slices, roasted pumpkin and cheeses, then place on the preheated stone or tray and bake for 5–6 minutes, or until the base is golden and crisp.

Sopressa salami pizza

Makes one 30 cm (12 inch) pizza

Peperonata
1 red, yellow and green capsicum (pepper)
500 ml (17 fl oz/2 cups) olive oil
1 large handful basil leaves
1 large handful flat-leaf (Italian) parsley
1 red onion, thinly sliced
3 garlic cloves, thinly sliced

Coarse semolina, for dusting
1 quantity pizza dough (page 12)
75 g (2½ oz/½ cup) grated mozzarella cheese
40 g (1½ oz) taleggio cheese
10 thin slices sopressa salami or mortadella
3 tablespoons shaved baby fennel
2 tablespoons lemon dressing (page 28)

To make the peperonata, roast the capsicums in a very hot oven until the skin blackens. Peel, seed and cut into long, thin strips. Heat the olive oil in a heavy-based saucepan over high heat and, when very hot, add the basil and parsley and cook for 40 seconds, or until crisp. Be careful not to burn the herbs. Using a slotted spoon, remove the fried herbs and drain on paper towel. Add the onion and garlic to the pan and cook over medium heat for 10 minutes, or until the onions are caramelised. Add the sliced roasted capsicum and fried herbs, combine well, then remove from the heat and cool, then season to taste. Peperonata will keep, refrigerated, for up to 1 week. Makes 750 ml (26 fl oz/3 cups).

Place a pizza stone or heavy-based oven tray in the oven and preheat to 250°C (500°F/Gas 9).

Lightly dust your workbench with semolina, then roll out the dough into a 30 cm (12 inch) round, place on a pizza tray and prick all over with a fork. Spread the base with 250 ml (9 fl oz/1 cup) of the peperonata, then scatter with the cheeses, place on the preheated stone or tray and bake for 5–8 minutes, or until the base is golden and crisp.

Remove from the oven, then place the sopressa over the top. Toss the shaved fennel with the lemon dressing, place on top of the pizza and serve.

Four-cheese pizza

Makes one 30 cm (12 inch) pizza

500 ml (17 fl oz/2 cups) vegetable oil
1 large handful basil leaves
1 large handful flat-leaf (Italian) parsley, plus 1 tablespoon chopped
Coarse semolina, for dusting
1 quantity pizza dough (page 12)
40 g (1^1/$_2$ oz) grated mozzarella cheese
35 g (1^1/$_4$ oz/^{1}/$_3$ cup) grated parmesan cheese
30 g (1 oz) gorgonzola dolce latte cheese
1 fig, cut into 6 wedges
40 g (1^1/$_2$ oz) buffalo mozzarella cheese, torn
2 tablespoons anchovy mayonnaise (page 28)
1 tablespoon extra virgin olive oil
1 tablespoon chilli confit (page 24)

Place a pizza stone or heavy-based oven tray in the oven and preheat to 250°C (500°F/Gas 9).

Heat the oil in a heavy-based saucepan over high heat and, when very hot, add the basil and parsley leaves and cook for 30 seconds, or until just crisp. Be careful not to burn the herbs. Using a slotted spoon, remove the fried herbs and drain on paper towel.

Lightly dust your workbench with semolina, then roll out the dough into a 30 cm (12 inch) round. Scatter the base with the grated mozzarella and half the parmesan and roll up tightly. Cut the roll into 2.5 cm (1 inch) thick slices, then place all the slices, cut side up, together on your workbench and re-roll into a 30 cm (12 inch) round. Place on a pizza tray and prick all over with a fork.

Combine the gorgonzola, remaining parmesan and the chopped parsley in a bowl, then spread over the base, place on the preheated pizza stone or tray and bake for 5–6 minutes, or until the base is golden and crisp.

Remove from the oven, top with the fig, buffalo mozzarella and the fried herbs, then drizzle with the anchovy mayonnaise, extra virgin olive oil and chilli confit, season to taste and serve.

Chilli prawn and salsa verde pizza

Makes one 30 cm (12 inch) pizza

200 g (7 oz) raw ocean king prawns (shrimp), peeled, deveined and cut lengthways into thirds
1 tablespoon chilli confit (page 24)
1 tablespoon garlic confit (page 24)
Coarse semolina, for dusting
1 quantity pizza dough (page 12)
1/2 quantity basic pizza sauce (page 18)
6 basil leaves
1 roma (plum) tomato, cut into 5 mm (1/4 inch) thick rounds
75 g (2 1/2 oz/1/2 cup) grated mozzarella cheese
1/2 small red capsicum (pepper), roasted until skin blackens, peeled, seeded and thinly sliced

Salsa verde
10 mint leaves
2 large handfuls flat-leaf (Italian) parsley
Juice of 1 lemon
3 anchovy fillets
80 ml (2 1/2 fl oz/1/3 cup) extra virgin olive oil

Combine the prawns, chilli confit and garlic confit in a bowl, cover and refrigerate overnight.

To make the salsa verde, put all the ingredients in a food processor, purée until smooth, then season to taste. Salsa verde will keep, refrigerated, for up to 1 week. Makes 250 ml (9 fl oz/1 cup).

Place a pizza stone or heavy-based oven tray in the oven and preheat to 250°C (500°F/Gas 9).

Lightly dust your workbench with semolina, then roll out the dough into a 30 cm (12 inch) round, place on a pizza tray and prick all over with a fork. Spread the base with the pizza sauce, then scatter with the basil, sliced tomato, mozzarella, prawns and sliced capsicum in that order. Place on the preheated stone or tray and bake for 5–8 minutes, or until the base is golden and crisp. Remove from the oven, drizzle with 2 tablespoons salsa verde and serve.

Italian meatball pizza

Makes one 30 cm (12 inch) pizza

Meatballs
50 g (1³/₄ oz) coarse minced (ground) pork
50 g (1³/₄ oz) coarse minced (ground) veal
2 teaspoons garlic confit (page 24)
3 tablespoons onion confit (page 22)
¹/₂ teaspoon chilli confit (page 24)
10 g (¹/₄ oz) fresh white breadcrumbs
1 tablespoon chopped flat-leaf (Italian) parsley
1 egg yolk
1 tablespoon olive oil

Coarse semolina, for dusting
1 quantity pizza dough (page 12)
¹/₂ quantity basic pizza sauce (page 18)
75 g (2¹/₂ oz/¹/₂ cup) grated mozzarella cheese
6 basil leaves
2 roma (plum) tomatoes, coarsely chopped
1 tablespoon chopped fresh oregano
3 cloves of confit garlic and 80 ml
    (2¹/₂ fl oz/¹/₃ cup) confit garlic oil (page 24)
35 g (1¹/₄ oz/¹/₃ cup) shaved parmesan cheese

To make the meatballs, combine all the ingredients except the oil in a bowl and season to taste, then roll the mixture into large marble-sized balls. Heat the oil in a large heavy-based frying pan over medium heat and cook the meatballs for 5–6 minutes, or until golden.

Place a pizza stone or heavy-based oven tray in the oven and preheat to 250°C (500°F/Gas 9).

Lightly dust your workbench with semolina, then roll out the dough into a 30 cm (12 inch) round, place on a pizza tray and prick all over with a fork. Spread the base with the pizza sauce, then scatter with the mozzarella, basil and meatballs. Place on the preheated stone or tray and bake for 5–8 minutes, or until the base is golden and crisp.

Meanwhile, put the tomatoes, oregano, garlic confit cloves and oil in a bowl and season to taste. Remove the pizza from the oven, top with the tomato salad, then scatter with the shaved parmesan and serve.

Eggplant caponata pizza

Makes one 30 cm (12 inch) pizza

Eggplant caponata
1/2 eggplant (aubergine) (cut lengthways)
80 ml (2 1/2 fl oz/1/3 cup) olive oil
1 tablespoon chopped flat-leaf (Italian) parsley
1 brown onion, finely chopped
1 roma (plum) tomato, seeded and chopped
2 teaspoons red wine vinegar

Eggplant purée
1 garlic clove, finely chopped
1 tablespoon soft unsalted butter

Coarse semolina, for dusting
1 quantity pizza dough (page 12)
6 basil leaves
1 roma (plum) tomato, cut into 5 mm
   (1/4 inch) thick rounds
50 g (1 3/4 oz/1/3 cup) grated mozzarella cheese
3 thin slices smoked mozzarella cheese

To make the caponata, peel the eggplant half then chop the skin into 5 mm (1/4 inch) pieces; reserve the inside flesh for the eggplant purée (following). Heat 3 tablespoons of the oil in a heavy-based frying pan over medium heat, add the eggplant skin and cook for 6 minutes, or until crisp. Pour the eggplant skin into a colander placed over a bowl, then return the drained oil to the pan. Add the parsley and half the onion and cook for 2 minutes, stir in the tomato and vinegar and season to taste. Eggplant caponata will keep, refrigerated, for up to 1 week. Makes 250 ml (9 fl oz/1 cup).

To make the eggplant purée, cut the reserved eggplant flesh into 1 cm (1/2 inch) pieces. Heat 1 tablespoon of the oil in a heavy-based frying pan over medium heat, add the garlic and the remaining chopped onion and cook for 5 minutes, or until soft. Add the chopped eggplant flesh and cook for another 5 minutes, or until very soft. Stir in the butter, then process the mixture in a food processor or blender until smooth and season to taste. Makes about 125 ml (4 fl oz/1/2 cup).

Place a pizza stone or heavy-based oven tray in the oven and preheat to 160°C (315°F/Gas 2–3). Cut the remaining eggplant half into very thin slices, lightly brush with oil, then place in a single layer on a baking tray, season to taste and bake for 8–10 minutes, or until tender.

Increase the oven temperature to 250°C (500°F/Gas 9). Lightly dust your workbench with semolina, then roll out the dough into a 30 cm (12 inch) round, place on a pizza tray and prick all over with a fork. Spread the base with 3 tablespoons eggplant purée, then top with the basil leaves, sliced tomato, baked eggplant slices and cheeses in that order. Place on the preheated stone or tray and bake for 5–8 minutes, or until the base is golden and crisp. Remove from the oven, spoon 125 ml (4 fl oz/1/2 cup) drained caponata over the top and serve.

Foot-long quail confit and roasted fig pizza

Makes one 30 cm (12 inch) oblong pizza

Quail confit
2 quails, boned
2 tablespoons sea salt
500 ml (17 fl oz/2 cups) olive oil

Coarse semolina, for dusting
1 quantity pizza dough (page 12)
$1/3$ quantity basic pizza sauce (page 18)
1 tablespoon onion confit (page 22)
1 tablespoon chilli confit (page 24)
2 tablespoons chopped flat-leaf (Italian) parsley
3 tablespoons grated buffalo mozzarella cheese
45 g ($1^1/2$ oz) gorgonzola dolce latte cheese
1 large or 2 small figs, sliced
Juice of 1 lemon
3 tablespoons grated Parmigiano Reggiano cheese

To make the quail confit, place them in a shallow dish, sprinkle over the salt, toss to coat, then refrigerate for 2 hours. Preheat the oven to 60°C (140°F). Rinse the quails, then pat dry with paper towel and place in a shallow ovenproof dish. Pour over the olive oil and bake for 3 hours, making sure the temperature of the oil does not exceed 60°C (140°F) (regulate with a thermometer). Remove the quails from the oven, leave in the fat until cool, then remove and tear into large pieces.

Place a pizza stone or heavy-based oven tray in the oven and preheat to 250°C (500°F/Gas 9).

Lightly dust your workbench with semolina, then roll out the dough lengthways into a 30 cm (12 inch) oblong, prick all over with a fork and place on a pizza tray. Spread the base with the pizza sauce, then scatter with the onion confit, chilli confit, parsley, mozzarella, gorgonzola, quail and figs in that order. Bring up the edges of the pizza to make a 2 cm ($3/4$ inch) border, covering the edges of the filling as you go, then, using your fingers, pinch the edges at 1 cm ($1/2$ inch) intervals. Place on the preheated stone or tray and bake for 6–8 minutes, or until the base is golden and crisp. Remove from the oven, squeeze over the lemon juice, sprinkle with the Parmigiano and serve.

Black pudding pizza

Makes one 30 cm (12 inch) pizza

1 tablespoon olive oil
1 small brown onion, thinly sliced
Coarse semolina, for dusting
1 quantity pizza dough (page 12)
$^1/_2$ quantity basic pizza sauce (page 18)
30 g (1 oz) thinly sliced smoked pork belly
40 g (1$^1/_2$ oz) grated smoked mozzarella cheese
20 g ($^3/_4$ oz) grated mozzarella cheese
1 tablespoon chopped flat-leaf (Italian) parsley
80 g (2$^3/_4$ oz) black pudding, thinly sliced
35 g (1$^1/_4$ oz/$^1/_3$ cup) shaved green apple
1 tablespoon crushed toasted walnuts
1$^1/_2$ tablespoons apple balsamic vinegar
2 teaspoons extra virgin olive oil

Heat the olive oil in a heavy-based frying pan over low heat, add the onion and cook for
4–5 minutes, or until soft.

Place a pizza stone or heavy-based oven tray in the oven and preheat to 250°C (500°F/Gas 9).

Lightly dust your workbench with semolina, then roll out the dough into a 30 cm (12 inch) round,
place on a pizza tray and prick all over with a fork. Spread the base with the pizza sauce, then
scatter with the smoked pork belly, onion, cheeses, parsley and black pudding in that order.
Season to taste, then place on the preheated stone or tray and bake for 5–8 minutes, or until
the base is golden and crisp.

Meanwhile, combine the shaved apple, walnuts, vinegar and oil and season to taste. Remove the
pizza from the oven, top with the apple salad and serve.

Filled river calamari pizza

Makes one 30 cm (12 inch) pizza

Filled calamari

40 g (1¹/₂ oz/¹/₃ cup) picked cooked crabmeat

3 tablespoons fresh white breadcrumbs

1 tablespoon chopped flat-leaf (Italian) parsley

1 egg yolk

2 river calamari hoods, about 10 cm (4 inches) long, rinsed

2 tablespoons olive oil

4 basil leaves

3 roma (plum) tomatoes, chopped

Coarse semolina, for dusting

1 quantity pizza dough (page 12)

75 g (2¹/₂ oz/¹/₂ cup) grated mozzarella cheese

1 large handful picked watercress sprigs

2 tablespoons lemon dressing (page 28)

1 tablespoon finely grated botarga or smoked mullet roe

Place a pizza stone or heavy-based oven tray in the oven and preheat to 160°C (315°F/Gas 2–3).

To make the filled calamari, combine the crabmeat, breadcrumbs, parsley and egg yolk in a bowl and season to taste. Fill the calamari hoods with the mixture and secure the ends with a toothpick. Heat the olive oil in a heavy-based ovenproof frying pan over high heat, add the calamari and cook until browned, then add the basil and chopped tomatoes, transfer the pan to the oven and bake for 25 minutes, or until the calamari is tender. Remove from the oven and cool the calamari in the pan.

Increase the oven temperature to 250°C (500°F/Gas 9).

Lightly dust your workbench with semolina, then roll out the dough into a 30 cm (12 inch) round, place on a pizza tray and prick all over with a fork. Spread the base with the calamari cooking sauce, then thinly slice the filled calamari and place over the top. Scatter the mozzarella over, season to taste, place on the preheated stone or tray and bake for 5–8 minutes, or until the base is golden and crisp. Remove from the oven. Combine the watercress and lemon dressing in a bowl, scatter over the pizza, then sprinkle with the grated botarga and serve.

Eggplant and spatchcock confit pizza

Makes one 30 cm (12 inch) pizza

1 large eggplant (aubergine), halved lengthways
1 tablespoon garlic confit (page 24)
1 tablespoon onion confit (page 22)
1 tablespoon chilli confit made with
  red chillies (page 24)
3 long fresh red chillies
Coarse semolina, for dusting
1 quantity pizza dough (page 12)
50 g (1³/₄ oz/¹/₃ cup) grated mozzarella cheese
30 g (1 oz/¹/₃ cup) grated chilli pecorino cheese
2 teaspoons chopped flat-leaf (Italian) parsley

Spatchcock confit
1 spatchcock, boned
500 ml (17 fl oz/2 cups) olive oil, plus extra,
  for drizzling
3 garlic cloves
4 basil or flat-leaf (Italian) parsley stalks

Preheat the oven to 60°C (140°F). To make the spatchcock confit, place all the ingredients in a casserole dish, making sure the spatchcock is covered with the oil, then bake for 2¹/₂ hours, ensuring the temperature of the oil does not exceed 60°C (140°F) (regulate with a thermometer). Remove from the oven, then leave the spatchcock to cool in the oil.

Increase the oven temperature to 140°C (275°F/Gas 1). Place the eggplant halves, cut side up, in an oven tray, spread with the combined confits, season, then bake for 1–1¹/₂ hours, or until the flesh is very soft. Scoop away the flesh, then mash with a fork and season to taste.

Meanwhile, heat a frying pan over high heat until very hot and just smoky, add the whole chillies and cook for 1 minute, or until the chillies are black and blistered all over. Cool, then peel, halve and seed the chillies and drizzle with olive oil.

Place a pizza stone or heavy-based oven tray in the oven and increase the heat to 250°C (500°F/Gas 9). Lightly dust your workbench with semolina, then roll out the dough into a 30 cm (12 inch) round, place on a pizza tray and prick all over with a fork. Spread the base with the eggplant purée, top with the halved chillies and the drained torn spatchcock, then scatter with the mozzarella, pecorino and parsley. Place on the preheated stone or tray and bake for 5–8 minutes, or until the base is golden and crisp.

Salmon belly with green olive tapenade pizza

Makes one 30 cm (12 inch) pizza

Coarse semolina, for dusting
1 quantity pizza dough (page 12)
$^1/_4$ quantity green olive tapenade (page 20)
65 g (2$^1/_4$ oz/$^1/_3$ cup) baked ricotta (available from Italian delicatessens), crumbled
120 g (4$^1/_4$ oz) salmon belly, thinly sliced
6 inside leaves of raddichio, torn
Juice of 1 lemon
1 tablespoon olive oil
2 tablespoons poor man's parmesan (page 26)

Place a pizza stone or heavy-based oven tray in the oven and preheat to 250°C (500°F/Gas 9).

Lightly dust your workbench with semolina, then roll out the dough into a 30 cm (12 inch) round, place on a pizza tray and prick all over with a fork. Spread the tapenade over the base, then scatter with the baked ricotta, place on the preheated stone or tray and bake for 5–8 minutes, or until the base is golden and crisp.

Remove from the oven. Combine the salmon, radicchio, lemon juice and olive oil in a bowl and season to taste. Scatter over the pizza, then sprinkle with the poor man's parmesan and serve.

Foie gras pizza

Makes one 30 cm (12 inch) pizza

2 egg yolks
15 g (¹/₂ oz) grated Parmigiano Reggiano cheese
1 tablespoon chopped flat-leaf (Italian) parsley
Coarse semolina, for dusting
1 quantity herb dough (page 14)
100 g (3¹/₂ oz) foie gras terrine
30 g (1 oz) minced (ground) pork and veal (taken from a skinned Italian sausage)
75 g (2¹/₂ oz/¹/₂ cup) grated mozzarella cheese
10 g (¹/₄ oz) fresh white Italian truffle, very thinly shaved

Place a pizza stone or heavy-based oven tray in the oven and preheat to 250°C (500°F/Gas 9).

Combine the egg yolks, Parmigiano and parsley in a bowl.

Lightly dust your workbench with semolina, then roll out the dough into a 30 cm (12 inch) round, place on a pizza tray and prick all over with a fork. Scatter the foie gras over the base. Roll the minced pork and veal into marble-sized balls and scatter over with the mozzarella. Place on the preheated pizza stone or tray and bake for 5–6 minutes, or until nearly cooked.

Open the oven door, pour the egg yolk, cheese and parsley mixture over the pizza and bake for another 2–3 minutes, or until the base is golden and crisp. Remove from the oven, scatter the white truffle over the top and serve.

Brawn celeriac salad pizza

Makes one 30 cm (12 inch) pizza

Coarse semolina, for dusting
1 quantity pizza dough (page 12)
125 ml (4 fl oz/$^1/_2$ cup) rich tomato ragu (page 18)
3 tablespoons grated mozzarella cheese
3 tablespoons grated parmesan cheese
60 g (2$^1/_4$ oz) brawn (head cheese), thinly sliced
Lemon wedges, to serve

Celeriac salad
1 small celeriac, peeled and julienned
$^1/_4$ quantity mayonnaise (page 28)
1 tablespoon chopped basil
Juice of $^1/_2$ lemon

Place a pizza stone or heavy-based oven tray in the oven and preheat to 250°C (500°F/Gas 9).

Lightly dust your workbench with semolina, then roll out the dough into a 30 cm (12 inch) round, place on a pizza tray and prick all over with a fork. Spread the base with the tomato ragu, then scatter with the combined cheeses, place on the preheated stone or tray and bake for 5–8 minutes, or until the base is golden and crisp.

Meanwhile, for the celeriac salad, combine all the ingredients in a bowl and season to taste. This should only be done while the pizza is cooking and not before. Remove the pizza from the oven, top with the brawn then the celeriac salad and serve with lemon wedges for squeezing over.

Chickpea purée and cotechino pizza

Makes one 30 cm (12 inch) pizza

Chickpea purée
2 tablespoons olive oil
1 small brown onion, finely chopped
1 garlic clove, finely chopped
60 g (2¼ oz) chickpeas, soaked overnight in cold water
400 ml (14 fl oz) chicken stock
1 small cotechino modena sausage

Coarse semolina, for dusting
1 quantity pizza dough (page 12)
40 g (1½ oz) grated smoked mozzarella cheese
20 g (¾ oz) taleggio cheese, torn

To make the chickpea purée, heat the olive oil in a heavy-based saucepan over low heat and cook the onion and garlic for 5 minutes, or until soft. Add the drained chickpeas, stock and cotechino and simmer very gently for 2 hours, or until the chickpeas are very tender and falling apart. Remove and reserve the cotechino, then purée the chickpeas in a food processor or blender until smooth. Push the chickpeas through a fine sieve and season to taste. The chickpea purée should not be too thin – if necessary, put it in a small saucepan and stir over low heat until thickened. Chickpea purée will keep, refrigerated, for up to 1 week. Makes 500 ml (17 fl oz/2 cups).

Place a pizza stone or heavy-based oven tray in the oven and preheat to 250°C (500°F/Gas 9).

Lightly dust your workbench with semolina, then roll out the dough into a 30 cm (12 inch) round, place on a pizza tray and prick all over with a fork. Spread the base with 4 tablespoons of the prepared chickpea purée. Cut the cotechino into eight 5 mm (¼ inch) thick slices, then scatter with the cheeses (remaining cotechino will keep, refrigerated, for up to 1 week). Place on the preheated pizza stone or tray and bake for 5–6 minutes, or until the base is golden and crisp.

Bresaola and basil pizza

Makes one 30 cm (12 inch) pizza

Coarse semolina, for dusting
1 quantity pizza dough (page 12)
$^1/_2$ quantity basic pizza sauce (page 18)
8 basil leaves
75 g (2$^1/_2$ oz/$^1/_2$ cup) grated mozzarella cheese
1 roma (plum) tomato, thinly sliced
6 slices of bresaola
$^1/_4$ quantity black olive tapenade (page 20)

Place a pizza stone or heavy-based oven tray in the oven and preheat to 250°C (500°F/Gas 9).

Lightly dust your workbench with semolina, then roll out the dough into a 30 cm (12 inch) round, place on a pizza tray and prick all over with a fork. Spread the pizza sauce over the base, then scatter with the basil, mozzarella and tomato slices. Place on the preheated stone or tray and bake for 5–8 minutes, or until the base is golden and crisp. Remove from the oven, top with the bresaola, then drizzle with the tapenade and serve.

Kingfish pizza

Makes one 30 cm (12 inch) pizza

75 g (2^1/$_2$ oz/^{2}/$_3$ cup) drained tinned artichoke hearts preserved in oil
1 tablespoon onion confit (page 22)
1 tablespoon garlic confit (page 24)
Coarse semolina, for dusting
1 quantity pizza dough (page 12)
2 tablespoons chopped flat-leaf (Italian) parsley
50 g (1^3/$_4$ oz/^{1}/$_3$ cup) grated mozzarella cheese
150 g (5^1/$_2$ oz) very thinly sliced kingfish
1 quantity lemon dressing (page 28)
65 g (2^1/$_4$ oz/^{1}/$_2$ cup) grated provolone picante cheese
Grilled lime halves, to serve

Place a pizza stone or heavy-based oven tray in the oven and preheat to 250°C (500°F/Gas 9).

Place the drained artichoke hearts, onion and garlic confits in a food processor, blend until smooth and season to taste.

Lightly dust your workbench with semolina, then roll out the dough into a 30 cm (12 inch) round, place on a pizza tray and prick all over with a fork. Spread the artichoke purée over the base, then scatter with the parsley and mozzarella. Place on the preheated stone or tray and bake for 5–8 minutes, or until the base is golden and crisp.

Remove from the oven, top with the sliced kingfish, drizzle over the lemon dressing, sprinkle with the provolone and serve with grilled lime halves for squeezing over.

Foot-long lamb pizza

Makes one 30 cm (12 inch) oblong pizza

120 g (4¹/₄ oz) lamb loin, trimmed of sinew and very finely chopped
2 tablespoons chopped flat-leaf (Italian) parsley
80 ml (2¹/₂ fl oz/¹/₃ cup) drained onion confit (page 22)
1 tablespoon chilli confit (page 24), finely chopped
Coarse semolina, for dusting
1 quantity pizza dough (page 12)
Olive oil, for brushing
Sea salt, to sprinkle
1 roma (plum) tomato, chopped
Juice of 1 lemon
1 tablespoon grated parmesan cheese

Combine the lamb, parsley, onion and chilli confits in a bowl and leave for 20 minutes.

Place a pizza stone or heavy-based oven tray in the oven and preheat to 250°C (500°F/Gas 9).

Lightly dust your workbench with semolina, then roll out the dough lengthways into a 30 cm (12 inch) oblong and place on a pizza tray. Spread the lamb mixture all over the base, then bring up the edges of the pizza to make a 2 cm (³/₄ inch) wide border, covering the edges of the filling as you go. Brush the edges with olive oil and sprinkle with sea salt, then place on the preheated stone or tray and bake for 6–8 minutes, or until the base is golden and crisp.

Remove from the oven, season the chopped tomato to taste and scatter over the top, sprinkle with parmesan, then drizzle with lemon juice and a little olive oil and serve.

Tuna tataki with green chilli purée pizza

Makes one 30 cm (12 inch) pizza

3 tablespoons sea salt
3 tablespoons coarsely ground black pepper
150 g (5^1/$_2$ oz) piece sashimi-grade tuna
Coarse semolina, for dusting
1 quantity pizza dough (page 12)
80 ml (2^1/$_2$ fl oz/^{1}/$_3$ cup) green chilli purée (page 24)
60 g (2^1/$_4$ oz) buffalo mozzarella cheese, torn

Bitter caramel
80 g (2^3/$_4$ oz/^{1}/$_3$ cup) caster (superfine) sugar
Juice of ^{1}/$_2$ lemon

Put the salt and pepper mixture on a plate, then roll the tuna in the mixture to coat evenly. Heat a nonstick frying pan over medium heat until smoking, then sear the tuna on all sides for 30 seconds. Immediately plunge the tuna into a bowl of iced water to stop it cooking. Remove and pat dry, then thinly slice the tuna.

To make the bitter caramel, put the sugar in a small heavy-based saucepan over low heat and cook, shaking the pan occasionally, until the sugar dissolves and a dark caramel forms, add the lemon juice, swirl the pan to combine, then remove from the heat and cool.

Place a pizza stone or heavy-based oven tray in the oven and preheat to 250°C (500°F/Gas 9).

Lightly dust your workbench with semolina, then roll out the dough into a 30 cm (12 inch) round, place on a pizza tray and prick all over with a fork. Spread the green chilli purée over the base, scatter with the mozzarella, then place on the preheated stone or tray and bake for 5–8 minutes, or until the base is golden and crisp. Remove from the oven, top with the tuna tataki, drizzle with a little bitter caramel and serve.

Pork and radicchio pizza

Makes one 30 cm (12 inch) pizza

1 double pork cutlet on the bone
1 garlic clove, finely chopped
3 tablespoons oregano leaves (stalks reserved)
Coarse semolina, for dusting
1 quantity pizza dough (page 12)
$^1/_2$ quantity basic pizza sauce (page 18)
2 tablespoons balsamic onions (page 22)
75 g ($2^1/_2$ oz/$^1/_2$ cup) grated mozzarella cheese
4 leaves radicchio
$1^1/_2$ tablespoons extra virgin olive oil
2 teaspoons balsamic vinegar
40 g ($1^1/_2$ oz) buffalo mozzarella cheese, torn

Preheat the oven to 140°C (275°F/Gas 1).

Season the pork cutlet, place in a small roasting pan, then scatter with the chopped garlic and reserved oregano stalks and bake for 3 hours, or until very tender. Remove from the oven, cool, then thinly shave the meat from the bone.

Place a pizza stone or heavy-based oven tray in the oven and increase the heat to 250°C (500°F/Gas 9).

Lightly dust your workbench with semolina, then roll out the dough into a 30 cm (12 inch) round, place on a pizza tray and prick all over with a fork. Spread the pizza sauce over the base, then scatter with oregano leaves, balsamic onions, mozzarella and shaved pork in that order. Place on the preheated pizza stone or tray and bake for 5–8 minutes, or until the base is golden and crisp.

Remove from the oven, toss the radicchio with the olive oil and balsamic vinegar, season and scatter over the pizza. Top with torn buffalo mozzarella and serve.

Pipi and sea urchin scroll pizza

Makes one 30 cm (12 inch) pizza scroll

300 g (10¹/₂ oz) pipis or clams, soaked in
    water for 30 minutes, changing water
    several times
80 ml (2¹/₂ fl oz/¹/₃ cup) dry white wine
100 g (3¹/₂ oz/¹/₂ cup) chopped
    green tomatoes
Coarse semolina, for dusting
1 quantity pizza dough (page 12)

45 g (1¹/₂ oz/¹/₂ cup) grated pecorino cheese
3 tablespoons grated mozzarella cheese
500 ml (17 fl oz/2 cups) olive oil
1 handful flat-leaf (Italian) parsley leaves
4 large garlic cloves, thinly sliced
16 sea urchins, meat removed
125 g (4¹/₂ oz/1 cup) cornflour (cornstarch)
2 teaspoons lemon dressing (page 28)

Heat a heavy-based saucepan over high heat until just smoking, add the pipis and wine, cover and shake for 3 minutes, or just until the shells open. Drain the pipis into a colander placed over a bowl, then return the cooking liquid to the pan and simmer over low heat for 5 minutes, or until reduced to 3 teaspoons. Add the chopped tomatoes, season lightly, then simmer for a further 5 minutes, or until a thick sauce has formed. Remove from the heat and stir in the parsley. Remove the meat from the pipis and discard the shells. Discard any unopened pipis.

Place a pizza stone or heavy-based oven tray in the oven and preheat to 250°C (500°F/Gas 9). Lightly dust your workbench with semolina, then roll out the dough into a 3 mm (¹/₈ inch) thick, 33 x 30 cm (13 x 12 inch) rectangle. Spread the dough with the pipi glaze, scatter with the pipis and cheeses, then, working from one long side, roll up the dough very tightly to make a scroll and fold in the ends to seal. Place the scroll on a pizza tray, then on the preheated stone or tray and bake for 8–12 minutes, or until golden and crisp.

Meanwhile, heat the oil in a heavy-based saucepan over medium heat and fry the parsley for 30 seconds, or until crisp, then remove with a slotted spoon and drain on paper towel. Add the garlic to the oil and cook until just golden (do not burn the garlic or it will become bitter). Remove with a slotted spoon and drain on paper towel. Reheat the oil until very hot, then dust the sea urchins with cornflour and fry for 10 seconds, or until golden. Remove with a slotted spoon, drain on paper towel and season to taste.

Remove the pizza from the oven, cut into 1.5 cm (¹/₂ inch) thick slices and lay on a plate. Scatter with the crisp parsley, garlic and fried sea urchins, drizzle over the lemon dressing and serve.

Spinach, feta and olive pizza

Makes one 30 cm (12 inch) pizza

Coarse semolina, for dusting
1 quantity pizza dough (page 12)
$^1/_2$ quantity basic pizza sauce (page 18)
150 g (5$^1/_2$ oz/3 cups) baby English spinach leaves, blanched and squeezed dry
3 tablespoons pitted manzanillo olives, halved
50 g (1$^3/_4$ oz/$^1/_3$ cup) crumbled Danish feta cheese
50 g (1$^3/_4$ oz/$^1/_3$ cup) grated mozzarella cheese
Chilli flakes, to taste
3 tablespoons semi-dried tomatoes
Juice of $^1/_2$ lemon

Place a pizza stone or heavy-based oven tray in the oven and preheat to 250°C (500°F/Gas 9).

Lightly dust your workbench with semolina, then roll out the dough into a 30 cm (12 inch) round, place on a pizza tray and prick all over with a fork. Spread the base with the pizza sauce, then place the spinach in small mounds all over the sauce, scatter with the olives, cheeses and chilli flakes. Place on the preheated stone or tray and bake for 5–6 minutes, or until the base is golden and crisp. Remove from the oven, scatter with the semi-dried tomatoes, drizzle with the lemon juice and serve.

Tuna pizza

Makes one 30 cm (12 inch) pizza

Coarse semolina, for dusting
1 quantity pizza dough (page 12)
$^1/_2$ quantity basic pizza sauce (page 18)
2 tablespoons chopped flat-leaf (Italian) parsley
100 g ($3^1/_2$ oz) tuna in olive oil, drained
Chilli flakes, to taste
75 g ($2^1/_2$ oz/$^1/_2$ cup) grated mozzarella cheese
2 tablespoons finely chopped green olives
1 tablespoon finely chopped red onion
1 tablespoon chilli confit (page 24)
2 tablespoons lemon juice
125 ml (4 fl oz/$^1/_2$ cup) extra virgin olive oil

Place a pizza stone or heavy-based oven tray in the oven and preheat to 250°C (500°F/Gas 9).

Lightly dust your workbench with semolina, then roll out the dough into a 30 cm (12 inch) round, place on a pizza tray and prick all over with a fork. Spread the pizza sauce over the base, then scatter with half the parsley and flake the tuna over the top. Sprinkle with the chilli flakes, then scatter with the mozzarella. Place on the preheated stone or tray and bake for 5–8 minutes, or until the base is golden and crisp.

While the pizza is cooking, combine the chopped olives, onion, chilli confit and remaining parsley in a bowl. Add the lemon juice and extra virgin olive oil and season to taste. Remove the pizza from the oven, spoon over the olive dressing and serve.

Braised goat with egg and summer truffle pizza

Makes one 30 cm (12 inch) oblong pizza

Braised goat
2 tablespoons olive oil
120 g (4¼ oz) goat leg meat, trimmed and cut into 1 cm (½ inch) pieces
1 tablespoon garlic confit (page 24)
1 tablespoon onion confit (page 22)
1 tablespoon chilli confit (page 24)
3 tablespoons cream

Coarse semolina, for dusting
1 quantity pizza dough (page 12)
100 g (3½ oz/½ cup) well-drained goat's curd
125 g (4½ oz) cherry tomatoes, sliced
1 egg
3 tablespoons chopped flat-leaf (Italian) parsley
3 tablespoons grated parmesan cheese
2 tablespoons summer truffles preserved in oil, drained and thinly shaved

To make the braised goat, heat the olive oil in a heavy-based frying pan over medium heat, add the goat meat and cook until browned. Add the garlic, onion and chilli confits, combine well, then add the cream, cover, reduce the heat to very low and cook gently for 1 hour, or until the meat is very tender. If necessary, add a little water during cooking if the mixture appears dry. Remove from the heat and cool.

Place a pizza stone or heavy-based oven tray in the oven and preheat to 250°C (500°F/Gas 9).

Lightly dust your workbench with semolina, then roll out the dough lengthways into a 30 cm (12 inch) oblong, place on a pizza tray and prick all over with a fork. Spread the base with the goat's curd, scatter with the tomato slices, then lightly beat the egg, parsley and parmesan together, season to taste and pour over the top. Bring up the edges of the pizza to make a 2 cm (¾ inch) border, covering the edges of the filling as you go. Place on the preheated stone or tray and bake for 6–8 minutes, or until the base is golden and crisp. Remove from the oven, scatter with shaved truffle and serve.

Lobster and caviar pizza

Makes one 30 cm (12 inch) pizza

Coarse semolina, for dusting
1 quantity pizza dough (page 12)
45 ml (1¹/₂ fl oz) shellfish glaze (page 20)
40 g (1¹/₂ oz) mascarpone cheese
1 small raw lobster tail, peeled and thinly sliced
1 tablespoon baby capers
2 tablespoons pitted green olives
3 tablespoons thinly sliced smoked eel
25 g (1 oz) grated mozzarella cheese
Grapeseed oil, for deep-frying
60 g (2¹/₄ oz) cleaned baby calamari, cut into 5 mm (¹/₄ inch) thick rings, tentacles reserved
40 g (1¹/₂ oz/¹/₃ cup) cornflour (cornstarch)
1 large handful picked watercress sprigs
2 tablespoons lemon dressing (page 28)
2 tablespoons Russian caviar

Place a pizza stone or heavy-based oven tray in the oven and preheat to 250°C (500°F/Gas 9).

Lightly dust your workbench with semolina, then roll out the dough into a 30 cm (12 inch) round, place on a pizza tray and prick all over with a fork. Spread the shellfish glaze over the base, then top with dollops of mascarpone, lobster, capers, olives, smoked eel and grated mozzarella in that order. Place on the preheated stone or tray and bake for 5–8 minutes, or until the base is golden and crisp.

Meanwhile, heat the oil in a deep-fryer or large, deep saucepan to 180°C (350°F), or until a cube of bread dropped in the oil browns in 15 seconds. Dust the calamari in cornflour, shaking off the excess, then deep-fry for 30 seconds, or until golden and crisp. Drain on paper towel and season to taste.

Remove the pizza from the oven. Toss the watercress sprigs with the lemon dressing and scatter over the pizza, then top with the fried calamari, sprinkle with the caviar and serve.

Salmon carpaccio pizza

Makes one 30 cm (12 inch) pizza

1 small red onion, cut into 5 mm
    ($^1/_4$ inch) thick rounds
250 ml (9 fl oz/1 cup) grapeseed oil
2 tablespoons capers in brine, rinsed
Coarse semolina, for dusting
1 quantity pizza dough (page 12)
$^1/_2$ quantity basic pizza sauce (page 18)
2 tablespoons chopped flat-leaf (Italian) parsley

75 g ($2^1/_2$ oz/$^1/_2$ cup) grated mozzarella cheese
120 g ($4^1/_4$ oz) skinless, pin-boned
    salmon fillet, cut into thin slices (see note)
2 tablespoons mascarpone cheese
1 large handful picked watercress sprigs
1 quantity lemon dressing (page 28)
1 tablespoon avruga caviar

Place a pizza stone or heavy-based oven tray in the oven and preheat to 250°C (500°F/Gas 9).

Lightly brush the onion rounds with oil, then cook on a barbecue char-grill plate or char-grill pan over medium heat for 5–6 minutes, or until golden and tender.

Heat the oil in a heavy-based frying pan over medium heat, add the capers and cook for 1–2 minutes, or until crisp. Remove with a slotted spoon and drain on paper towel.

Lightly dust your workbench with semolina, then roll out the dough into a 30 cm (12 inch) round, place on a pizza tray and prick all over with a fork. Spread the pizza sauce over the base, scatter with the chopped parsley, grilled onion and mozzarella in that order. Place on the preheated stone or tray and bake for 5–8 minutes, or until the base is golden and crisp.

Remove from the oven, top with the sliced salmon, then the fried capers and dollops of mascarpone. Toss the watercress with the lemon dressing, scatter over the top and sprinkle with the caviar and serve.

Note: If you have trouble slicing the salmon very thinly, place the slices between two pieces of baking paper and beat gently with a rolling pin.

Mushroom pizza

Makes one 30 cm (12 inch) pizza

Mushroom purée
15 button mushrooms, sliced
1 small brown onion, finely chopped
3 tablespoons chopped flat-leaf (Italian) parsley
3 garlic cloves, finely chopped

2 tablespoons olive oil
200 g (7 oz) field mushrooms, thinly sliced
Coarse semolina, for dusting
1 quantity pizza dough (page 12)
6 basil leaves
40 g (1¹/₂ oz) taleggio cheese
40 g (1¹/₂ oz) buffalo mozzarella cheese
75 g (2¹/₂ oz/¹/₂ cup) grated mozzarella cheese

To make the mushroom purée, heat 1 tablespoon of the olive oil in a heavy-based frying pan over medium heat, then add the mushrooms, onion, parsley and 2 of the chopped garlic cloves and cook for 10 minutes, or until soft. Put the mushroom mixture in a food processor and purée until smooth, cool, then season to taste.

Heat the remaining olive oil in a heavy-based frying pan and cook the sliced field mushrooms and remaining garlic, tossing over high heat until golden and the juices have evaporated. Remove from the heat and season to taste.

Place a pizza stone or heavy-based oven tray in the oven and preheat to 250°C (500°F/Gas 9).

Lightly dust your workbench with semolina, then roll out the dough into a 30 cm (12 inch) round, place on a pizza tray and prick all over with a fork. Spread the base with the mushroom purée, then scatter with the basil, fried mushrooms and cheeses in that order. Place on the preheated stone or tray and bake for 5–8 minutes, or until the base is golden and crisp.

Confit cuttlefish and pesto pizza scroll

Makes one 30 cm (12 inch) pizza scroll

120 g (4^1/$_4$ oz) cleaned cuttlefish
250 ml (9 fl oz/1 cup) olive oil
3 flat-leaf (Italian) parsley sprigs
1 head of garlic, halved
Coarse semolina, for dusting
1 quantity pizza dough (page 12)
^{1}/$_4$ quantity pesto (page 26)
75 g (2^1/$_2$ oz/^{1}/$_2$ cup) grated mozzarella cheese

Using a sharp knife, thinly slice the cuttlefish on the diagonal, then place in a heavy-based saucepan with the olive oil, parsley and garlic. Place a thermometer in the oil and cook over very low heat, making sure the temperature doesn't exceed 40°C (104°F), for 2 hours, or until the cuttlefish is very tender. Cool the cuttlefish in the oil, then drain and reserve the oil to make another confit or for pan-frying fish.

Place a pizza stone or heavy-based oven tray in the oven and preheat to 250°C (500°F/Gas 9).

Lightly dust your workbench with semolina, then roll out the dough into a 3 mm (^{1}/$_8$ inch) thick, 33 x 30 cm (13 x 12 inch) rectangle. Spread the pesto over the dough, then scatter with the mozzarella and drained cuttlefish. Working from one long side, roll up the dough very tightly to make a scroll and fold in the ends to seal. Place the scroll on a pizza tray, then on the preheated stone or tray and bake for 8–12 minutes, or until golden and crisp. Remove from the oven, cut into 1.5 cm (^{5}/$_8$ inch) thick slices and serve.

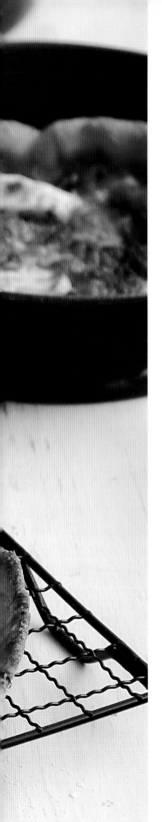

Pizza pies

Today, you'll find traditional pizza pies eaten in the country towns of Sicily. Those recipes tend to use a thick crust as a base and are often topped with a thick dough lid, enclosing the whole pizza and making it easy to eat on the run. I've adapted those traditional recipes by using a much thinner crust and leaving the lid off – I think the presentation and taste is better this way. All the pizza pies in this chapter are cooked in a 12 cm (4$\frac{1}{2}$ inch) round, 2.5 cm (1 inch) deep pizza pan and use the same amount of dough as the other standard pizzas in this book.

Salt cod, green olive and caper pizza pies

Makes four 12 cm (4^1/$_2$ inch) pizza pies

300 g (10^1/$_2$ oz) dried salt cod (bacalao), soaked in cold water for 2 days,
    changing the water twice per day
1 litre (35 fl oz/4 cups) sparkling mineral water
Coarse semolina, for dusting
4 quantities pizza dough (page 12)
2 quantities basic pizza sauce (page 18)
85 g (3 oz/^{2}/$_3$ cup) pitted green olives
70 g (2^1/$_2$ oz/^{1}/$_3$ cup) baby capers in salt, rinsed
4 tablespoons onion confit (page 22)
^{1}/$_3$ quantity garlic confit (page 24)
2 tablespoons chilli confit (page 24)
150 g (5^1/$_2$ oz/1 cup) grated mozzarella cheese
^{3}/$_4$ quantity poor man's parmesan (page 26)

Put the drained salt cod and the mineral water in a small saucepan over low heat and simmer for 20 minutes, or until the fish starts to fall off the bone. Drain, discard the bones and skin, then coarsely flake the flesh.

Place two pizza stones or heavy-based oven trays in the oven and preheat to 250°C (500°F/Gas 9).

Lightly dust your workbench with semolina, then roll out each portion of dough into a 14 cm (5^1/$_2$ inch) round, and line the base and halfway up the sides of four 12 cm (4^1/$_2$ inch) round, 2.5 cm (1 inch) deep, pizza pans. Divide the salt cod among the pizza bases, then spoon over the pizza sauce. Scatter with the olives, capers, onion, garlic and chilli confits and mozzarella in that order, then place on the preheated stones or trays and bake for 8–10 minutes, or until golden and crisp. Remove from the oven, sprinkle over the poor man's parmesan and serve.

Pork belly and mushroom pizza pies

Makes four 12 cm (4¹/₂ inch) pizza pies

80 ml (2¹/₂ fl oz/¹/₃ cup) olive oil
650 g (1 lb 7 oz) boneless pork belly, skin discarded, cut into 8 pieces
2 tablespoons garlic confit (page 24)
2 tablespoons onion confit (page 22)
6 roma (plum) tomatoes, chopped
1 large handful basil leaves
500 ml (17 fl oz/2 cups) sparkling mineral water
270 g (9¹/₂ oz/3 cups) mixed mushrooms, including button, Swiss brown and small field, sliced
2 garlic cloves, thinly sliced
Coarse semolina, for dusting
4 quantities pizza dough (page 12)
80 g (2³/₄ oz) taleggio cheese
20 g (³/₄ oz) parmesan cheese
40 g (1¹/₂ oz) grated mozzarella cheese

Heat 2 tablespoons of the oil in a heavy-based saucepan over medium heat and cook the pork in batches until browned. Add the garlic and onion confit, tomatoes, basil and mineral water, bring to the boil, then reduce the heat to low and simmer gently for 2 hours, or until the meat is very tender and falling apart and the sauce is thick and reduced.

Heat the remaining oil in a heavy-based frying pan and cook the mushrooms over high heat for 3–4 minutes, or until just tender. Add the sliced garlic and cook for another minute, then add the mushroom mixture to the pork mixture and season to taste.

Place two pizza stones or heavy-based oven trays in the oven and preheat to 250°C (500°F/Gas 9).

Lightly dust your workbench with semolina, then roll out each portion of dough into a 14 cm (5¹/₂ inch) round and line the base and halfway up the sides of four 12 cm (4¹/₂ inch) round, 2.5 cm (1 inch) deep, pizza pans. Divide the pork mixture among the pans (making sure you don't add too much sauce or the base will go soggy), then scatter with the cheeses. Place the pans on the preheated stones or trays and bake for 8–10 minutes, or until golden and crisp.

Spicy garlic prawn pizza pies

Makes four 12 cm (4¹/₂ inch) pizza pies

1 large red onion, peeled and cut into 5 mm (¹/₄ inch) thick rounds
Olive oil, for brushing
400 g (14 oz) raw prawns (shrimp), peeled, deveined and coarsely chopped
¹/₃ quantity red chilli confit (page 24)
¹/₃ quantity garlic confit (page 24)
4 tablespoons onion confit (page 22)
Coarse semolina, for dusting
4 quantities pizza dough (page 12)
1 quantity basic pizza sauce (page 18)
150 g (5¹/₂ oz/1 cup) grated mozzarella cheese
³/₄ quantity poor man's parmesan (page 26)
4 tablespoons chopped flat-leaf (Italian) parsley
Lemon wedges, to serve

Lightly brush the onion rounds with oil, then cook on a barbecue char-grill plate or char-grill pan over medium heat for 5–6 minutes, or until golden and tender.

Combine the chopped prawns and the chilli, garlic and onion confits in a bowl and leave for 10 minutes.

Place two pizza stones or heavy-based oven trays in the oven and preheat to 250°C (500°F/Gas 9).

Lightly dust your workbench with semolina, then roll out each portion of dough into a 14 cm (5¹/₂ inch) round and line the base and halfway up the sides of four 12 cm (4¹/₂ inch) round, 2.5 cm (1 inch) deep, pizza pans. Spread the bases with the pizza sauce, then scatter with the marinated prawns, mozzarella, char-grilled onions, parsley and poor man's parmesan in that order. Place the pans on the preheated stones or trays and bake for 8–10 minutes, or until golden and crisp. Serve with lemon wedges for squeezing over.

Braised lamb shank and fresh pea pizza pies

Makes four 12 cm (4¹/₂ inch) pizza pies

Braised lamb shanks
2 tablespoons olive oil
4 lamb shanks
1 small brown onion, finely chopped
1 celery stalk, finely chopped
250 ml (9 fl oz/1 cup) dry white wine
1 tablespoon chopped flat-leaf (Italian) parsley
310 g (11 oz/2 cups) fresh peas
125 ml (4 fl oz/¹/₂ cup) beef stock

Coarse semolina, for dusting
4 quantities pizza dough (page 12)
120 g (4¹/₄ oz) buffalo mozzarella cheese, torn
30 g (1 oz/¹/₃ cup) grated pecorino cheese

Preheat the oven to 140°C (275°F/Gas 1).

To make the braised lamb shanks, heat the oil in a flameproof casserole dish over high heat and cook the shanks until browned. Remove from the pan, reduce the heat to low, add the onion and celery and cook for 5–6 minutes, or until translucent. Return the shanks to the pan, add the wine and bring to a simmer. Cover the pan tightly with foil and bake in the oven for 1 hour, then add the peas and bake for another hour, or until the meat is falling off the bone. Remove the shanks from the sauce, discard the bones and shred the meat, then return the meat to the pan and simmer over low heat until the sauce thickly coats the back of a spoon.

Place two pizza stones or heavy-based oven trays in the oven and preheat to 250°C (500°F/Gas 9).

Lightly dust your workbench with semolina, then roll out each portion of dough into a 14 cm (5¹/₂ inch) round and line the base and halfway up the sides of four 12 cm (4¹/₂ inch) round, 2.5 cm (1 inch) deep, pizza pans. Spread the bases with 4 tablespoons each of the lamb shank mixture, scatter with the mozzarella, then place the pans on the preheated stones or trays and bake for 8–10 minutes, or until golden and crisp. Remove from the oven, sprinkle with the grated pecorino and serve.

Rich tomato ragu with bone marrow and summer truffle pizza pies

Makes four 12 cm (4¹/₂ inch) pizza pies

Coarse semolina, for dusting
4 quantities pizza dough (page 12)
¹/₂ quantity rich tomato ragu (page 18)
1 handful flat-leaf (Italian) parsley, chopped
75 g (2¹/₂ oz/¹/₂ cup) grated mozzarella cheese
80 g (2³/₄ oz) fontina cheese, sliced
300 g (10¹/₂ oz) marrow bones, soaked in cold water for 3 hours, marrow pushed
    out of the bone and cut into 5 mm (¹/₄ inch) thick slices
30 g (1 oz) summer truffles preserved in olive oil, drained

Place two pizza stones or heavy-based oven trays in the oven and preheat to 250°C (500°F/Gas 9).

Lightly dust your workbench with semolina, then roll out each portion of dough into a 14 cm (5¹/₂ inch) round and line the base and halfway up the sides of four 12 cm (4¹/₂ inch) round, 2.5 cm (1 inch) deep, pizza pans. Spread each base with the tomato ragu, scatter with the parsley and cheeses, then place the bone marrow over the top. Place the pans on the preheated pizza stones or trays and bake for 8–10 minutes, or until golden and crisp. Remove from the oven, shave the truffles over the top and serve.

Rabbit and balsamic onion pizza pies

Makes four 12 cm (4^1/$_2$ inch) pizza pies

Rabbit casserole
1 tablespoon olive oil
1 farmed white rabbit, jointed
1 small brown onion, finely chopped
1 small carrot, finely chopped
1 celery stalk, finely chopped
70 g (2^1/$_2$ oz/^{1}/$_2$ cup) finely chopped pancetta
2 handfuls flat-leaf (Italian) parsley, chopped
125 ml (4 fl oz/^{1}/$_2$ cup) dry red wine
250 ml (9 fl oz/1 cup) beef stock
2 roma (plum) tomatoes, chopped

Coarse semolina, for dusting
4 quantities pizza dough (page 12)
1 quantity balsamic onions (page 22)
75 g (2^1/$_2$ oz/^{1}/$_2$ cup) grated mozzarella cheese
30 g (1 oz/^{1}/$_3$ cup) grated pecorino cheese,
    plus extra, to serve

Preheat the oven to 170°C (325°F/Gas 3). To make the rabbit casserole, heat the olive oil in a flameproof casserole dish over medium heat and cook the rabbit pieces until browned all over. Remove from the pan, then add the onion, carrot and celery and cook for 5 minutes, or just until soft. Add the pancetta and parsley and cook for a further 2 minutes, then return the rabbit pieces to the pan, pour in the wine and bring to the boil. Add the stock, then place a piece of baking paper over the surface, cover with a lid and bake for 2 hours, or until the meat is very tender. Remove from the oven and, when cool enough to handle, remove the rabbit pieces from the sauce, discard the bones and shred the meat. Return the meat to the casserole, add the tomatoes, bring to a simmer, then remove from the heat, season to taste and cool.

Place two pizza stones or heavy-based oven trays in the oven and preheat to 250°C (500°F/Gas 9). Lightly dust your workbench with semolina, then roll out each portion of dough into a 14 cm (5^1/$_2$ inch) round and line the base and halfway up the sides of four 12 cm (4^1/$_2$ inch) round, 2.5 cm (1 inch) deep, pizza pans. Spread 250 ml (9 fl oz/1 cup) of rabbit casserole over each base, then scatter with the balsamic onions and the cheeses. Place the pans on the preheated stones or trays and bake for 8–10 minutes, or until golden and crisp. Sprinkle each pizza pie with a little grated pecorino and serve.

My cheese pizza pies

Makes four 12 cm (4¹/₂ inch) pizza pies

Béchamel
20 g (³/₄ oz) butter
20 g (³/₄ oz) plain (all-purpose) flour
200 ml (7 fl oz) milk

Coarse semolina, for dusting
4 quantities pizza dough (page 12)
65 g (2¹/₄ oz/1¹/₂ cup) grated provolone picante cheese
120 g (4¹/₄ oz) gorgonzola dolce latte cheese
50 g (1³/₄ oz/¹/₂ cup) grated parmesan cheese
140 g (5 oz) tallegio cheese, torn
2 tablespoons chopped flat-leaf (Italian) parsley
120 g (4¹/₄ oz) buffalo mozzarella cheese, torn
³/₄ quantity poor man's parmesan (page 26)

To make the béchamel, melt the butter in a small heavy-based saucepan over medium heat, add the flour and stir for 1–2 minutes, or until the mixture becomes sandy in colour. Whisking continuously, gradually pour in the milk and whisk until thick and well combined, then reduce the heat to very low and simmer, stirring frequently, for 15 minutes. Remove from the heat and season to taste.

Place two pizza stones or heavy-based oven trays in the oven and preheat to 250°C (500°F/Gas 9).

Lightly dust your workbench with semolina, then roll out each portion of dough into a 14 cm (5¹/₂ inch) round and line the base and halfway up the sides of four 12 cm (4¹/₂ inch) round, 2.5 cm (1 inch), deep pizza pans. Spread each base with a quarter of the béchamel. Put the provolone, gorgonzola, parmesan and tallegio in a bowl, add the parsley and stir until coarsely combined. Spread the cheese mixture over the top of the béchamel, place the pans on the preheated stones or trays and bake for 8–10 minutes, or until golden and crisp. Remove from the oven, scatter with the buffalo mozzarella and the poor man's parmesan and serve.

Garlic marron with shellfish glaze pizza pies

Makes four 12 cm (4¹/₂ inch) pizza pies

12 live marron, or small crayfish
750 ml (26 fl oz/3 cups) olive oil
²/₃ quantity garlic confit (page 24)
¹/₃ quantity chilli confit (page 24)
4 tablespoons onion confit (page 22)
2 large handfuls flat-leaf (Italian) parsley, chopped
200 g (7 oz/1 cup) chopped roma (plum) tomatoes
Coarse semolina, for dusting
4 quantities pizza dough (page 12)
¹/₂ quantity shellfish glaze (page 20)
150 g (5¹/₂ oz/1 cup) grated mozzarella cheese
¹/₃ quantity poor man's parmesan (page 26)

Place the marron in the freezer for 30 minutes to put them to sleep, then drop them in a large saucepan of boiling salted water and cook for 20 seconds. Drain and refresh the marron in iced water, then drain again and peel, reserving 4 heads with claws attached to top the pizzas, if desired. Cut the tails into 1 cm (¹/₂ inch) pieces – the meat should only be half cooked.

Heat the olive oil in a heavy-based saucepan over low heat, add the garlic, chilli and onion confits and cook for 30 seconds, then add the chopped marron and parsley and cook for a further 2 minutes. Add the chopped tomato and cook for another minute, then remove from the heat and pour into a sieve placed over a bowl.

Place two pizza stones or heavy-based oven trays in the oven and preheat to 250°C (500°F/Gas 9).

Lightly dust your workbench with semolina, then roll out each portion of dough into a 14 cm (5¹/₂ inch) round and line the base and halfway up the sides of four 12 cm (4¹/₂ inch) round, 2.5 cm (1 inch) deep, pizza pans. Divide the drained garlic marron among the pans, drizzle each with the shellfish glaze, then scatter with the mozzarella. If using the heads, place them on top. Place the pans on the preheated stones or trays and bake for 8–10 minutes, or until golden and crisp. Remove from the oven, sprinkle with the poor man's parmesan and serve.

Note: You can use the cooled marron cooking oil to make a delicious spicy mayonnaise.

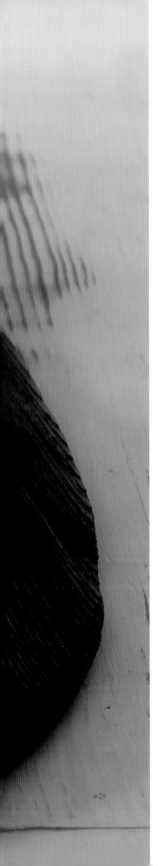

Calzone

Like many of the pizzas in this book, calzone have been around for a very long time. Traditionally, this pizza style was favoured by Italian farmers, who would take partly cooked calzone to work for lunch with fillings taken from the meal the night before – the fillings would stay fresher as they were enclosed in the pastry. At lunch, the calzone were cooked on a open fire – and always enjoyed with some wine. Today, we tend to use only the best filling ingredients, rather than leftovers, but you can ensure the legacy continues by also enjoying these with wine.

Sautéed cauliflower calzone

Makes one 30 cm (12 inch) calzone

1 tablespoon olive oil
150 g (5^1/$_2$ oz) cauliflower florets, cut into 1 cm (^{1}/$_2$ inch) pieces
70 g (2^1/$_2$ oz/^{1}/$_2$ cup) finely chopped leek, white part only
1 roma (plum) tomato, chopped
1 tablespoon chopped chives
1 tablespoon pine nuts, toasted
35 g (1^1/$_4$ oz/^{1}/$_3$ cup) grated parmesan cheese
1 egg, lightly beaten
Coarse semolina, for dusting
1 quantity pizza dough (page 12)

Heat the olive oil in a heavy-based saucepan over medium heat, add the cauliflower and leek and cook for 6–8 minutes, or until tender. Add the tomato and cook for a further 5 minutes, then add the chives, pine nuts and the parmesan, combine well and season to taste. Remove from the heat, cool until just warm, then stir in the egg.

Place a pizza stone or heavy-based oven tray in the oven and preheat to 190°C (375°F/Gas 5).

Lightly dust your workbench with semolina, then roll out the dough into a 30 cm (12 inch) round and place on a pizza tray. Spread the cauliflower mixture over one side of the base, leaving a 2 cm (^{3}/$_4$ inch) border, then fold the other half over the filling and pinch the edges together at 1 cm (^{1}/$_2$ inch) intervals to prevent any juices escaping. Place on the preheated stone or tray and bake for 8–10 minutes, or until golden and crisp.

Braised pork skin calzone

Makes one 30 cm (12 inch) calzone

Braised pork skin
2 tablespoons olive oil
1 brown onion, finely chopped
1 garlic clove, finely chopped
40 g (1½ oz) fresh cleaned white pork skin (ask your butcher), cut into 1 cm (½ inch) pieces
1 small pork shank
½ celery stalk, finely chopped
250 ml (9 fl oz/1 cup) tinned chopped Italian tomatoes
250 ml (9 fl oz/1 cup) chicken stock
6 basil leaves
1 fresh red bird's eye chilli, split

Coarse semolina, for dusting
1 quantity pizza dough (page 12)
50 g (1¾ oz/⅓ cup) chopped buffalo mozzarella cheese
3 tablespoons finely grated pecorino cheese

To make the braised pork skin, heat the olive oil in a heavy-based saucepan over low heat and cook the onion and garlic for 6–8 minutes, or until soft. Add the remaining ingredients, bring to the boil, then reduce the heat to very low, cover and simmer for 2 hours, or until the meat is almost falling off the bone. Remove from the heat and leave until cool, then remove the meat from the shanks, discard the bones and return the meat to the sauce. Season to taste, cool, remove the chilli, then refrigerate until cold. Braised pork skin will keep, frozen, for up to 3 months. Makes 375 ml (13 fl oz/1½ cups).

Place a pizza stone or heavy-based oven tray in the oven and preheat to 190°C (375°F/Gas 5).

Lightly dust your workbench with semolina, then roll out the dough into a 30 cm (12 inch) round and place on a pizza tray. Spread 4 tablespoons of the braised pork skin over half the base, scatter with the cheeses, then fold the other half over the filling and pinch the edges together at 1 cm (½ inch) intervals to prevent the juices escaping. Place on the preheated stone or tray and bake for 8–10 minutes, or until golden and crisp.

Tripe parmigiana calzone

Makes one 30 cm (12 inch) calzone

2 tablespoons olive oil
150 g (5^1/$_2$ oz) honeycomb tripe, cut into 1 x 3 cm (^{1}/$_2$ x 1^1/$_4$ inch) pieces
1 fresh long red chilli, halved, seeded and finely chopped
^{1}/$_2$ choko (chayote), peeled and cut into 1 cm (^{1}/$_2$ inch) pieces
2 tablespoons chopped basil
1 sebago potato, peeled and cut into 2 cm (^{3}/$_4$ inch) pieces
250 ml (9 fl oz/1 cup) tinned chopped Italian tomatoes
2 tablespoons grated chilli pecorino cheese
60 g (2^1/$_4$ oz) buffalo mozzarella cheese, chopped
35 g (1^1/$_4$ oz/^{1}/$_3$ cup) grated parmesan cheese
20 g (^{3}/$_4$ oz) butter
Coarse semolina, for dusting
1 quantity pizza dough (page 12)

Heat the olive oil in a heavy-based saucepan over high heat, add the tripe, chilli, choko, basil and potato and cook for 6–8 minutes, or until the potato is light golden. Add the tomatoes, reduce the heat to as low as possible, cover and simmer for 2 hours, or until the tripe is very tender. Remove from the heat, stir in the cheeses and butter, season to taste and cool.

Place a pizza stone or heavy-based oven tray in the oven and preheat to 190°C (375°F/Gas 5).

Lightly dust your workbench with semolina, then roll out the dough into a 30 cm (12 inch) round and place on a pizza tray. Spread the tripe mixture over half the base, leaving a 2 cm (^{3}/$_4$ inch) border, then fold the other half over the filling and pinch the edges together at 1 cm (^{1}/$_2$ inch) intervals to prevent the juices from escaping. Place on the preheated stone or tray and bake for 8–10 minutes, or until golden and crisp.

Duck ragu calzone

Makes one 30 cm (12 inch) calzone

Duck ragu
2 tablespoons olive oil
1 brown onion, finely chopped
1 tablespoon finely chopped carrot
1 tablespoon finely chopped celery
1 tablespoon finely chopped garlic
3 duck leg quarters, skin removed
2 tablespoons finely chopped flat-leaf (Italian) parsley
250 ml (9 fl oz/1 cup) dry red wine
400 g (14 oz) tinned chopped Italian tomatoes

Coarse semolina, for dusting
1 quantity pizza dough (page 12)
30 g (1 oz/$^1/_3$ cup) grated pecorino picante cheese
40 g (1$^1/_2$ oz) buffalo mozzarella cheese, torn

Preheat the oven to 160°C (315°F/Gas 2–3).

To make the duck ragu, heat the olive oil in a heavy-based saucepan over medium heat, add the onion, carrot, celery and garlic and cook for 5 minutes, or until soft. Add the duck and cook for 10 minutes, or until browned, then add the parsley and wine and simmer until nearly evaporated. Add the tomatoes, cover and bake for 3 hours, or until the meat is nearly falling off the bone. Remove the bones, shred the meat, then return it to the sauce and season to taste. Duck ragu will keep, frozen, for up to 3 months and also makes a delicious sauce for fresh pasta. Makes 1.25 litres (44 fl oz/5 cups).

Place a pizza stone or heavy-based oven tray in the oven and preheat to 190°C (375°F/Gas 5).

Lightly dust your workbench with semolina, then roll out the dough into a 30 cm (12 inch) round and place on a pizza tray. Spread 250 ml (9 fl oz/1 cup) of the duck ragu over one side of the base, leaving a 2 cm ($^3/_4$ inch) border, sprinkle with the cheeses, then fold the other side over the filling and pinch the edges together at 1 cm ($^1/_2$ inch) intervals to prevent juices escaping. Place on the preheated stone or tray and bake for 8–10 minutes, or until golden and crisp.

Lambs' brain and mushroom calzone

Makes one 30 cm (12 inch) calzone

2 tablespoons olive oil
80 g (2³/₄ oz) cleaned lambs' brains (ask your butcher)
80 g (2³/₄ oz) small field mushrooms, thinly sliced
40 g (1¹/₂ oz/¹/₃ cup) chopped sweet potato, steamed until par-cooked
Coarse semolina, for dusting
1 quantity pizza dough (page 12)
2 hard-boiled eggs, quartered
1 tablespoon chopped flat-leaf (Italian) parsley
60 g (2¹/₄ oz) buffalo mozzarella cheese, torn
30 g (1 oz/¹/₃ cup) grated pecorino cheese

Place a pizza stone or heavy-based oven tray in the oven and preheat to 190°C (375°F/Gas 5).

Heat the olive oil in a heavy-based frying pan over medium–high heat, add the brains and cook for 40 seconds, or until browned. Remove from the pan, then add the mushrooms and sweet potato and cook for 8 minutes, or until the sweet potato is soft. Remove the pan from the heat and season to taste.

Lightly dust your workbench with semolina, then roll out the dough into a 30 cm (12 inch) round and place on a pizza tray. Spread the mushroom mixture over one side of the base, top with the eggs, parsley, brains, buffalo mozzarella and pecorino in that order. Fold the other side over the filling and pinch the edges together at 1 cm (¹/₂ inch) intervals to prevent juices escaping. Place on the preheated stone or tray and bake for 8–10 minutes, or until golden and crisp.

Braised lentil and cotechino calzone

Makes one 30 cm (12 inch) calzone

2 tablespoons olive oil
1 small carrot, finely chopped
1 small brown onion, finely chopped
1 small cotechino modena sausage, blanched
95 g (3$\frac{1}{2}$ oz/$\frac{1}{2}$ cup) puy lentils
375 ml (13 fl oz/1$\frac{1}{2}$ cups) chicken stock
40 g (1$\frac{1}{2}$ oz) taleggio cheese
3 tablespoons grated pecorino cheese
Coarse semolina, for dusting
1 quantity pizza dough (page 12)

Heat the olive oil in a heavy-based saucepan over low heat, add the carrot and onion and cook for 6–8 minutes, or until tender. Cut 150 g (5$\frac{1}{2}$ oz) cotechino into 5 mm ($\frac{1}{4}$ inch) thick slices, then add to the vegetables with the lentils and stock and simmer very gently for 1$\frac{1}{2}$ hours, or until the lentils are tender. Remove from the heat, cool, then fold in the cheeses and season to taste.

Place a pizza stone or heavy-based oven tray in the oven and preheat to 190°C (375°F/Gas 5).

Lightly dust your workbench with semolina, then roll out the dough into a 30 cm (12 inch) round and place on a pizza tray. Spread the lentil and cotechino mixture over one side of the base, then fold the other side over the filling and pinch the edges together at 1 cm ($\frac{1}{2}$ inch) intervals to prevent juices escaping. Place on the preheated stone or tray and bake for 8–10 minutes, or until golden and crisp.

Italian savoury pie

Makes one 30 cm (12 inch) calzone

1 tablespoon olive oil
100 g (3^1/$_2$ oz/^{1}/$_2$ cup) coarse minced (ground) pork and fennel
   (taken from a skinned Italian sausage)
2 tablespoons chopped flat-leaf (Italian) parsley
75 g (2^1/$_2$ oz/^{1}/$_3$ cup) sliced drained artichoke hearts marinated in oil
Coarse semolina, for dusting
1 quantity pizza dough (page 12)
1 hard-boiled egg, coarsely chopped
50 g (1^3/$_4$ oz/^{1}/$_2$ cup) shaved provolone dolce cheese
70 g (2^1/$_2$ oz/^{1}/$_2$ cup) thinly shaved fennel
1 tablespoon lemon dressing (page 28)

Heat the olive oil in a heavy-based frying pan over medium heat, add the minced pork and cook, breaking the meat apart with a wooden spoon, for 3 minutes, or until browned. Add the parsley and artichokes, season to taste and remove from the heat.

Place a pizza stone or heavy-based oven tray in the oven and preheat to 190°C (375°F/Gas 5).

Lightly dust your workbench with semolina, then roll out the dough into a 30 cm (12 inch) round and place on a pizza tray. Spread the pork mixture over half the base, leaving a 2 cm (^{3}/$_4$ inch) border, scatter with the egg and provolone, then fold over the other side to cover the filling and pinch the edges together at 1 cm (^{1}/$_2$ inch) intervals to prevent juices escaping. Place on the preheated stone or tray and bake for 8–10 minutes, or until golden and crisp. Remove from the oven, toss the fennel with the lemon dressing and serve on the side.

Mum's octopus calzone

Makes one 30 cm (12 inch) calzone

80 ml (2$^1/_2$ fl oz/$^1/_3$ cup) olive oil
2 garlic cloves, thinly sliced
400 g (14 oz) cleaned baby octopus
3 tablespoons chopped flat-leaf (Italian) parsley
400 g (14 oz) tinned Italian tomatoes, drained
3 tablespoons poor man's parmesan (page 26)
Coarse semolina, for dusting
1 quantity pizza dough (page 12)
30 g (1 oz/$^1/_3$ cup) grated pecorino cheese

Heat the olive oil in a heavy-based frying pan over high heat, add the garlic and octopus and cook for 15 minutes. Add the parsley and tomatoes and cook for a further 60 minutes, or until the tomatoes start to separate from the oil. Remove from the heat, stir in the poor man's parmesan and season to taste.

Place a pizza stone or heavy-based oven tray in the oven and preheat to 190°C (375°F/Gas 5).

Lightly dust your workbench with semolina, then roll out the dough into a 30 cm (12 inch) round and place on a pizza tray. Spread the octopus mixture over one side of the base, sprinkle with the pecorino, then fold the other side over the filling and pinch the edges together at 1 cm ($^1/_2$ inch) intervals to prevent juices escaping. Place on the preheated stone or tray and bake for 8–10 minutes, or until golden and crisp.

Snapper and cherry tomato calzone

Makes one 30 cm (12 inch) calzone

2 tablespoons olive oil
100 g (3^1/$_2$ oz) boneless snapper fillet, skin on
60 g (2^1/$_4$ oz) cherry tomatoes
8 basil leaves
1 tablespoon sparkling mineral water
20 g (^{3}/$_4$ oz) sebago potato, peeled and cut into 1 cm (^{1}/$_2$ inch) pieces, lightly blanched
20 g (^{3}/$_4$ oz) soft butter
3 tablespoons ricotta cheese
50 g (1^3/$_4$ oz/^{1}/$_2$ cup) shaved provolone picante cheese
Coarse semolina, for dusting
1 quantity pizza dough (page 12)

Heat the olive oil in a heavy-based frying pan over medium heat, add the snapper, skin side down, and cook, without moving, for 3 minutes, or until the skin is crisp. Turn the fish over, add the tomatoes, basil, mineral water and potato, season lightly and simmer for a further 5 minutes, or until the fish is just cooked through. Remove the pan from the heat, gently flake the fish with a fork, then stir in the butter. Cool, then stir in the ricotta and season to taste.

Place a pizza stone or heavy-based oven tray in the oven and preheat to 190°C (375°F/Gas 5).

Lightly dust your workbench with semolina, then roll out the dough into a 30 cm (12 inch) round and place on a pizza tray. Spread the snapper mixture over one side of the base, sprinkle with the provolone, then fold the other side over the filling and pinch the edges together at 1 cm (^{1}/$_2$ inch) intervals to prevent juices escaping. Place on the preheated stone or tray and bake for 8–10 minutes, or until golden and crisp.

Smoked trout calzone

Makes one 30 cm (12 inch) calzone

8 local black mussels, cleaned
2 fresh red bird's eye chillies, seeded and finely chopped
1 anchovy fillet
30 g (1 oz) broccolini, blanched and finely chopped
100 g (3$^1/_2$ oz) skinless smoked rainbow trout, bones removed, flesh flaked
50 g (1$^3/_4$ oz/$^1/_2$ cup) provolone picante cheese
40 g (1$^1/_2$ oz) buffalo mozzarella cheese, torn
Coarse semolina, for dusting
1 quantity pizza dough (page 12)

Heat a small heavy-based saucepan over medium–high heat until very hot, add the mussels, cover and shake for 2–3 minutes, or just until the shells open. Pour the mussels into a colander placed over a bowl, remove the meat and discard the shells. Return the mussel cooking liquid to the pan, add the chillies, anchovy, broccolini and trout and stir over low heat for 5 minutes, or until fragrant and well combined. Remove from the heat, then fold in the provolone and season to taste.

Place a pizza stone or heavy-based oven tray in the oven and preheat to 190°C (375°F/Gas 5).

Lightly dust your workbench with semolina, then roll out the dough into a 30 cm (12 inch) round and place on a pizza tray. Spread the mixture over one side of the base, sprinkle with the mozzarella, then fold the other side over the filling and pinch the edges together to prevent any juices escaping. Place on the preheated stone or tray and bake for 8–10 minutes, or until golden and crisp.

Kids' pizzas

I've always thought children should join in the fun of making pizza – and which kid doesn't love pizza? The pizzas in this chapter are smaller in diameter but big on creativity – and with flavours that everyone will be sure to love. Get them started with making the dough – just be prepared for the major flour mess that's sure to follow. Be sure to also let the kids scatter the ingredients over the tops of the pizzas. This is also a good time to introduce the little ones to some ingredients they may not know or recognise – by secretly slipping them in if you have to.

Roast chicken and salad mini pizzas

Makes eight 6 cm (2 ¹/₂ inch) pizzas

2 chicken thighs
2 tablespoons chopped fresh mixed herbs, including basil, flat-leaf (Italian) parsley and coriander
3 garlic cloves, bruised
2 tablespoons olive oil, plus extra, for drizzling
2 teaspoons plain (all-purpose) flour
125 ml (4 fl oz/¹/₂ cup) chicken stock or water
Coarse semolina, for dusting
1 quantity pizza dough (page 12)
3 tablespoons grated mozzarella cheese
3 tablespoons grated tasty cheddar cheese
1 small handful finely shredded iceberg lettuce

Combine the chicken, herbs, garlic and oil in a bowl, cover and refrigerate for 1 hour.

Preheat the oven to 180°C (350°F/Gas 4). Put the chicken in a small heavy-based roasting tin, season and roast for 20 minutes, or until cooked through. Remove the chicken from the dish, then place the dish over low heat, add the flour and stir with a wooden spoon for 2 minutes. Gradually stir in the stock or water, then simmer for 5 minutes, or until thickened slightly. Remove from the heat, strain and season to taste.

Place a pizza stone or heavy-based oven tray in the oven and increase the oven temperature to 250°C (500°F/Gas 9).

Lightly dust your workbench with semolina, then roll out the dough into a 30 cm (12 inch) round. Using a 6 cm (2¹/₂ inch) cutter, cut out 8 rounds from the dough, place on a pizza tray and prick all over with a fork. Thinly slice the chicken, then divide among the bases, sprinkle with the cheeses, drizzle with a little gravy, then place on the preheated stone or tray and bake for 6 minutes, or until golden and crisp. Remove from the oven, scatter with the shredded lettuce, drizzle with a little extra olive oil and serve.

Sausage and mash mini pizzas

Makes eight 6 cm (2 ½ inch) pizzas

Mashed potato
1 large desiree potato
20 g (¾ oz) butter
2 tablespoons cream

2 tablespoons olive oil
1 white onion, thinly sliced
Coarse semolina, for dusting
1 quantity pizza dough (page 12)
2 Italian pork sausages, blanched, then cut into 5 mm (¼ inch) thick slices
3 tablespoons grated mozzarella cheese
3 tablespoons grated tasty cheddar cheese
Barbecue sauce, for drizzling

To make the mashed potato, cook the potato in boiling water until tender, drain then mash. Add the butter and cream, season to taste and combine well.

Meanwhile, heat the olive oil in a small heavy-based frying pan over medium heat, add the onion and cook for 5 minutes, or until golden, then season to taste.

Place a pizza stone or heavy-based oven tray in the oven and preheat to 250°C (500°F/Gas 9).

Lightly dust your workbench with semolina, then roll out the dough into a 30 cm (12 inch) round. Using a 6 cm (2½ inch) cutter, cut out eight rounds from the dough, place on a pizza tray and prick all over with a fork. Divide the sausage slices and onions among the bases, then scatter with the cheeses and top each with 1 tablespoon of the mashed potato. Place on the preheated stone or tray and bake for 6 minutes, or until golden and crisp. Drizzle with barbecue sauce and serve.

Double-smoked ham and cheese mini pizzas

Makes eight 6 cm (2 1/2 inch) pizzas

Coarse semolina, for dusting
1 quantity pizza dough (page 12)
1/3 quantity basic pizza sauce (page 18)
3 tablespoons grated mozzarella cheese
3 tablespoons grated tasty cheddar cheese
70 g (2 1/2 oz/1/2 cup) shredded double-smoked ham
1 tablespoon chopped flat-leaf (Italian) parsley
1 tablespoon onion confit (page 22)

Place a pizza stone or heavy-based oven tray in the oven and preheat to 250°C (500°F/Gas 9).

Lightly dust your workbench with semolina, then roll out the dough into a 30 cm (12 inch) round. Using a 6 cm (2 1/2 inch) cutter, cut out 8 rounds from the dough, place on a pizza tray and prick all over with a fork. Spread the bases with pizza sauce, then sprinkle with the cheeses, ham, parsley and onion confit in that order. Place on the preheated stone or tray and bake for 6 minutes, or until golden and crisp.

Mushroom and lamb mini pizzas

Makes eight 6 cm (2 $^1/_2$ inch) pizzas

1 lamb loin, trimmed of sinew
1$^1/_2$ tablespoons olive oil
40 g (1$^1/_2$ oz) butter
200 g (7 oz) button mushrooms, thinly sliced
Coarse semolina, for dusting
1 quantity pizza dough (page 12)
2 tablespoons grated mozzarella cheese
2 tablespoons grated tasty cheddar cheese
$^1/_4$ quantity pesto (page 26)

Brush the lamb with a little oil and season to taste. Heat a heavy-based frying pan over high heat, add the lamb and cook for 1 minute, or until browned all over. Remove from the pan and leave for 10 minutes, then cut into thin slices.

Meanwhile, heat the butter and remaining oil in a large heavy-based frying pan over medium–high heat, add the mushrooms, season to taste and cook for 5–6 minutes, or until tender.

Place a pizza stone or heavy-based oven tray in the oven and preheat to 250°C (500°F/Gas 9).

Lightly dust your workbench with semolina, then roll out the dough into a 30 cm (12 inch) round. Using a 6 cm (2$^1/_2$ inch) cutter, cut out 8 rounds from the dough, place on a pizza tray and prick all over with a fork. Scatter with the mushrooms and cheeses, season to taste, then place on the preheated stone or tray and bake for 6 minutes, or until golden and crisp. Remove from the oven, top with a little lamb and a small dollop of pesto and serve.

Cheese, tomato and basil mini pizzas

Makes eight 6 cm (2 ¹/₂ inch) pizzas

Coarse semolina, for dusting
1 quantity pizza dough (page 12)
¹/₂ quantity basic pizza sauce (page 18)
2 roma (plum) tomatoes, thinly sliced
3 tablespoons grated mozzarella cheese
3 tablespoons grated tasty cheddar cheese
6 basil leaves

Place a pizza stone or heavy-based oven tray in the oven and preheat to 250°C (500°F/Gas 9).

Lightly dust your workbench with semolina, then roll out the dough into a 30 cm (12 inch) round. Using a 6 cm (2¹/₂ inch) cutter, cut out 8 rounds from the dough, place on a pizza tray and prick all over with a fork. Spread the pizza sauce over the bases, then place 2 tomato slices over the top, scatter with the combined cheeses and top with a basil leaf. Place on the preheated stone or tray and bake for 6 minutes, or until golden and crisp.

Sausage roll scroll

Makes 8 pieces

Coarse semolina, for dusting
1 quantity pizza dough (page 12)
$^1/_2$ quantity basic pizza sauce (page 18)
3 tablespoons grated mozzarella cheese
3 tablespoons grated tasty cheddar cheese
8 basil leaves
200 g (7 oz/1 cup) combined minced (ground) beef and pork (or either)
1 tablespoon garlic confit (page 24)
1 tablespoon onion confit (page 22)
1 tablespoon chopped flat-leaf (Italian) parsley
1 egg yolk

Place a pizza stone or heavy-based oven tray in the oven and preheat to 250°C (500°F/Gas 9).

Lightly dust your workbench with semolina, then roll out the dough into a 30 cm (12 inch) round. Spread the pizza sauce over the base, leaving a 2 cm ($^3/_4$ inch) border, sprinkle the cheeses and basil leaves over the top. Put the minced meat, garlic and onion confits, parsley and egg yolk in a bowl, season and combine well. Break up the meat mixture into large marble-sized pieces and scatter over the top of the pizza, then roll up tightly to make a log. Cut the log into 2 cm ($^3/_4$ inch) thick slices and place, seam side down, on a pizza tray, then on the preheated stone or tray and bake for 6–8 minutes, or until golden and crisp.

Savoury beef mini pizza pies

Makes eight 4 cm (1 1/2 inch) pizza pies

2 tablespoons olive oil
200 g (7 oz) braising beef, cut into 1 cm (1/2 inch) pieces
1 tablespoon garlic confit (page 24)
1 tablespoon onion confit (page 22)
125 ml (4 fl oz/1/2 cup) beef stock
3 teaspoons cornflour (cornstarch)
Coarse semolina, for dusting
1 quantity pizza dough (page 12)
2 tablespoons chopped thyme
3 tablespoons grated mozzarella cheese
3 tablespoons grated tasty cheddar cheese

Heat the oil in a heavy-based saucepan over medium–high heat, add the beef and cook until browned all over. Add the confits and stock, reduce the heat to very low, cover and simmer for 1 hour, or until the meat is very tender. Combine the cornflour with 1 tablespoon of water to make a smooth paste, then add to the pan with the thyme, combine well and simmer very gently until the sauce has thickened. The mixture should not be too wet or the pizzas will be soggy.

Place a pizza stone or heavy-based oven tray in the oven and preheat to 250°C (500°F/Gas 9).

Lightly dust your workbench with semolina, then roll out the dough into a 30 cm (12 inch) round. Using a 6 cm (2 1/2 inch) cutter, cut out 8 rounds from the dough, then use to line the base and sides of eight 4 cm (1 1/2 inch) quiche tins. Fill the moulds with the beef mixture, sprinkle with the cheeses, then place on the preheated stone or tray and bake for 6–8 minutes, or until golden and crisp.

Ham and pineapple mini pizzas

Makes eight 6 cm (2 $^1/_2$ inch) pizzas

100 g (3$^1/_2$ oz) piece fresh pineapple
Coarse semolina, for dusting
1 quantity pizza dough (page 12)
$^1/_2$ quantity basic pizza sauce (page 18)
1 tablespoon chopped flat-leaf (Italian) parsley
75 g (2$^1/_2$ oz/$^1/_2$ cup) grated mozzarella cheese
100 g (3$^1/_2$ oz/$^2/_3$ cup) double-smoked ham, cut freehand off the bone

Preheat the oven to 180°C (350°F/Gas 4). Put the pineapple in a small roasting tin and bake for 20 minutes, or until the outside begins to brown, then cool and thinly slice.

Place a pizza stone or heavy-based oven tray in the oven and preheat to 250°C (500°F/Gas 9).

Lightly dust your workbench with semolina, then roll out the dough into a 30 cm (12 inch) round. Using a 6 cm (2$^1/_2$ inch) cutter, cut out 8 rounds from the dough, place on a pizza tray and prick all over with a fork. Spread the pizza sauce over the bases, then scatter with the parsley, pineapple, mozzarella and ham in that order. Place the tray on the preheated pizza stone or tray and bake for 6 minutes, or until golden and crisp.

Steak with egg and bacon mini pizzas

Makes eight 6 cm (2 $\frac{1}{2}$ inch) pizzas

2 tablespoons olive oil
1 brown onion, thinly sliced
100 g (3$\frac{1}{2}$ oz) piece fillet steak
Coarse semolina, for dusting
1 quantity pizza dough (page 12)
$\frac{1}{2}$ quantity basic pizza sauce (page 18)
3 tablespoons grated mozzarella cheese
70 g (2$\frac{1}{2}$ oz) rindless bacon, shredded
1 egg
1 tablespoon grated parmesan cheese
1 tablespoon chopped flat-leaf (Italian) parsley

Heat half the oil in a heavy-based frying pan over low heat, add the onion, season to taste and cook for 6 minutes, or until lightly caramelised.

Meanwhile, season the meat to taste, heat the remaining olive oil in a heavy-based frying pan over high heat and cook the steak for 30 seconds on each side, or until browned but still slightly pink. Leave the steak for 10 minutes, then cut against the grain into thin slices.

Place a pizza stone or heavy-based oven tray in the oven and preheat to 250°C (500°F/Gas 9).

Lightly dust your workbench with semolina, then roll out the dough into a 30 cm (12 inch) round. Using a 6 cm (2$\frac{1}{2}$ inch) cutter, cut out 8 rounds from the dough, place on a pizza tray and prick all over with a fork. Spread the bases with pizza sauce, then sprinkle with the mozzarella, onion and bacon. Lightly beat the egg, parmesan and parsley together, season to taste, then drizzle over the pizzas. Place on the preheated stone or tray and bake for 6 minutes, or until golden and crisp. Remove from the oven, top with the steak slices and serve.

Dessert pizzas

Dessert pizza – it has always been said – is not 'real' pizza. It's true that sweet pizzas may not be 'traditional', but one type – the hazelnut chocolate pizza – has been popular in Italy for many generations. And, why not? Imagine sitting around munching through deliciously sweet things on a crispy crust – it doesn't sound too bad to me. I love dessert pizzas, as do my family and my patrons too. Following are some of the simplest and tastiest sweet pizzas you will ever eat.

My favourite chocolate pizza

Makes two 15 cm (6 inch) pizzas

115 g (4 oz/^{1}/$_2$ cup) caster (superfine) sugar
1 tablespoon lemon juice
Coarse semolina, for dusting
1 quantity sweet pizza dough (page 14) or pizza dough (page 12)
100 g (3^1/$_2$ oz) chocolate hazelnut spread
2 tablespoons mascarpone cheese
12 maraschino cherries, halved
12 bite-sized pieces plain Turkish delight
40 g (1^1/$_2$ oz/^{1}/$_3$ cup) chopped unsalted pistachio nuts
Vanilla bean ice cream, to serve

Heat the sugar and lemon juice in a small heavy-based saucepan over low heat, shaking the pan occasionally, until the sugar melts and becomes a light caramel. Pour the toffee onto a baking tray lined with baking paper and tilt until it spreads very thinly. Leave it to set.

Place a pizza stone or heavy-based oven tray in the oven and preheat to 250°C (500°F/Gas 9).

Lightly dust your workbench with semolina, then roll out the dough into two 15 cm (6 inch) rounds or free-form shapes, place on a pizza tray and prick all over with a fork. Spread the bases with the chocolate hazelnut spread, then top with small dollops of mascarpone and scatter over the cherries. Place on the preheated stone or tray and bake for 5 minutes, or until the bases are golden and crisp.

Remove from the oven, scatter with the Turkish delight and pistachios. Break the toffee into chards, scatter over the top and serve with vanilla bean ice cream.

Variation: Spread the bases with the chocolate hazelnut spread, then bake for 5 minutes. Fold 3 chopped strawberries through one large scoop of vanilla bean ice cream, place on top of each of the pizzas, then scatter with 50 g (1^3/$_4$ oz/^{1}/$_3$ cup) shaved white chocolate each and serve.

Poached pear and almond pizza

Makes two 15 cm (6 inch) pizzas

Poached pears
500 ml (17 fl oz/2 cups) red wine
230 g (8 oz/1 cup) caster (superfine) sugar
1 cinnamon stick
$^1/_4$ star anise
3 cloves
2 corella pears, or other small, firm pears

2 egg whites
115 g (4 oz/$^1/_2$ cup) caster (superfine) sugar
155 g (5$^1/_2$ oz/1 cup) blanched almonds, finely ground
25 g (1 oz) white chocolate, finely chopped
Coarse semolina, for dusting
1 quantity sweet pizza dough (page 14) or pizza dough (page 12)
6 small scoops of vanilla bean ice cream
2 tablespoons flaked almonds, toasted
Icing (confectioners') sugar, for dusting

To make the poached pears, put the wine, sugar and spices in a saucepan over medium heat and bring to a simmer. Peel and core the pears, put in the wine mixture, cover with a piece of baking paper, then reduce the heat to low and simmer gently for 8 minutes. Remove the pan from the heat, cool the pears in the liquid, then remove and cut lengthways into 3 cm (1$^1/_4$ inch) thick slices.

Meanwhile, to make the almond mixture, whisk the egg whites until soft peaks form, then gradually add the sugar and whisk until thick and glossy. Add the ground almonds and mix well.

Place a pizza stone or heavy-based oven tray in the oven and preheat to 250°C (500°F/Gas 9).

Lightly dust your workbench with semolina, then roll out the dough into two 15 cm (6 inch) rounds or free-form shapes, place on a pizza tray and prick all over with a fork. Spread the bases with 3 tablespoons almond mixture, sprinkle with the chocolate and sliced pear. Place the pizzas on the preheated stone or tray and bake for 5 minutes, or until the bases are golden and crisp. Remove from the oven, top with the ice cream, scatter with toasted almonds, dust with icing sugar and serve.

Banana split pizza

Makes two 15 cm (6 inch) pizzas

Caramel sauce
50 g (1³/₄ oz) caster (superfine) sugar
1 tablespoon lemon juice
25 g (1 oz) butter
1 teaspoon cream

Coarse semolina, for dusting
1 quantity sweet pizza dough (page 14) or pizza dough (page 12)
2 bananas, thinly sliced
Vanilla bean ice cream, to serve
Hundreds and thousands, for sprinkling

To make the caramel sauce, put the sugar and lemon juice in a heavy-based saucepan over low heat and cook, shaking pan occasionally, until it becomes a light caramel. Add the butter and cream and whisk to combine well, then remove from the heat.

Place a pizza stone or heavy-based oven tray in the oven and preheat to 250°C (500°F/Gas 9).

Lightly dust your workbench with semolina, then roll out the dough into two 15 cm (6 inch) rounds or free-form shapes, place on a pizza tray and prick all over with a fork. Scatter the bananas over the bases then place on the preheated stone or tray and bake for 4–6 minutes, or until the bases are golden and crisp. Remove the pizzas from the oven, top with the ice cream, drizzle with the caramel sauce, sprinkle with hundreds and thousands and serve.

Cherry and almond pizza

Makes two 15 cm (6 inch) pizzas

Coarse semolina, for dusting
1 quantity sweet pizza dough (page 14) or pizza dough (page 12)
100 g (3^1/$_2$ oz) marzipan
100 g (3^1/$_2$ oz) pitted cherries
2 tablespoons pouring custard (available from supermarkets), plus extra, to serve
Almond or vanilla bean ice cream, to serve
1 tablespoon slivered almonds, toasted

Place a pizza stone or heavy-based oven tray in the oven and preheat to 250°C (500°F/Gas 9).

Lightly dust your workbench with semolina, then roll out the dough into two 15 cm (6 inch) rounds or free-form shapes, place on a pizza tray and prick all over with a fork. Place the marzipan in a small saucepan and stir over low heat until it reaches spreading consistency, then spread over the bases. Combine the cherries and custard, spread over the marzipan, then place on the preheated stone or tray and bake for 5 minutes, or until the bases are golden and crisp. Remove from the oven, drizzle with a little extra custard, top with the ice cream and toasted almonds and serve.

Peaches and cream pizza

Makes two 15 cm (6 inch) pizzas

Coarse semolina, for dusting
1 quantity sweet pizza dough (page 14) or pizza dough (page 12)
2 teaspoons honey
3 tablespoons mascarpone cheese
120 g (4¹/₄ oz/1 cup) well-drained stewed peaches
3 tablespoons thick cream
6 chocolate chip cookies, coarsely crumbled

Place a pizza stone or heavy-based oven tray in the oven and preheat to 250°C (500°F/Gas 9).

Lightly dust your workbench with semolina, then roll out the dough into two 15 cm (6 inch) rounds or free-form shapes, place on a pizza tray and prick all over with a fork. Combine the honey and mascarpone until smooth, then spread over the bases and top with the stewed peaches. Place the pizzas on the preheated stone or tray and bake for 5 minutes, or until the bases are golden and crisp. Remove from the oven, top with the combined cream and crumbled cookies and serve.

Warm italian meringue and vincotto grapes pizza

Makes two 15 cm (6 inch) pizzas

20 g ($^3/_4$ oz) butter
90 g ($3^1/_4$ oz/$^1/_2$ cup) seedless red grapes, peeled
125 ml (4 fl oz/$^1/_2$ cup) vincotto
3 egg whites
1 tablespoon caster (superfine) sugar
Coarse semolina, for dusting
1 quantity sweet pizza dough (page 14) or pizza dough (page 12)

Melt the butter in a small heavy-based saucepan over medium heat, add the grapes and cook for 3 minutes, or until just tender. Remove the grapes, add the vincotto and simmer until reduced by half. Return the grapes to the pan, toss to combine well, then remove from the heat and cool.

Place a pizza stone or heavy-based oven tray in the oven and preheat to 250°C (500°F/Gas 9).

Using electric beaters, whisk the egg whites until stiff peaks have nearly formed. Meanwhile, put the sugar and 1 tablespoon water in a small saucepan and bring to the boil. Whisking continuously, gradually add the hot syrup to the beaten egg whites and whisk until stiff and glossy.

Lightly dust your workbench with semolina, then roll out the dough into two 15 cm (6 inch) rounds or free-form shapes, place on a pizza tray and prick all over with a fork. Spread the bases with the Italian meringue, then place on the preheated stone or tray and bake for 4–6 minutes, or until the bases are golden and crisp, making sure the meringue doesn't burn. Remove from the oven, scatter with the vincotto grapes and serve.

Blueberry, coconut and chocolate pizza

Makes two 15 cm (6 inch) pizzas

Chocolate liqueur zabaglione
2 egg yolks
1 teaspoon caster (superfine) sugar
3 tablespoons chocolate liqueur

Coarse semolina, for dusting
1 quantity sweet pizza dough (page 14) or pizza dough (page 12)
150 g (5^1/$_2$ oz) coconut chocolate bar
40 g (1^1/$_2$ oz) blueberries
2 tablespoons shaved white chocolate

To make the chocolate liqueur zabaglione, whisk the egg yolks and sugar in a heatproof bowl set over a saucepan of simmering water until thick and pale, then add the liqueur and whisk until the mixture leaves a trail.

Place a pizza stone or heavy-based oven tray in the oven and preheat to 250°C (500°F/Gas 9).

Lightly dust your workbench with semolina, then roll out the dough into two 15 cm (6 inch) rounds or free-form shapes, place on a pizza tray and prick all over with a fork. Crumble the coconut chocolate bar evenly over the bases, then scatter with the blueberries, place on the preheated stone or tray and bake for 4–6 minutes, or until the bases are golden and crisp. Remove from the oven, drizzle with the zabaglione, scatter with the chocolate shavings and serve.

Milk chocolate and marshmallow coffee froth pizza

Makes two 15 cm (6 inch) pizzas

Coarse semolina, for dusting
1 quantity sweet pizza dough (page 14) or pizza dough (page 12)
100 g (3¹/₂ oz) milk chocolate, melted
2 tablespoons mascarpone cheese
7 marshmallows, halved
125 ml (4 fl oz/¹/₂ cup) soy milk
2 tablespoons very strong espresso coffee

Place a pizza stone or heavy-based oven tray in the oven and preheat to 250°C (500°F/Gas 9).

Lightly dust your workbench with semolina, then roll out the dough into two 15 cm (6 inch) rounds or free-form shapes, place on a pizza tray and prick all over with a fork. Drizzle the melted chocolate over the bases, then dollop the marscapone over the top, place on the preheated stone or tray and bake for 4 minutes. Scatter the marshmallows over the tops, then bake for another 1–2 minutes, or until the bases are golden and crisp.

Meanwhile, put the soy milk in a small saucepan over low heat and heat to 50°C (120°F). Add the coffee and stir over low heat until just tepid, then, using a stick blender, whizz the milk mixture until foamy. Remove the pizzas from the oven, drizzle with the coffee froth and serve.

Index